Beginning to R

Janet Morris & Linda Mort

Bright Ideas
FOR Early Years

Published by Scholastic Publications Ltd,
Villiers House, Clarendon Avenue,
Leamington Spa, Warwickshire
CV32 5PR

© 1992 Scholastic Publications
Reprinted 1993, 1994, 1995

Written by Janet Morris and Linda Mort
Edited by Juliet Gladston
Designed by Anna Oliwa
Illustrations by Emma Brown
Photographs by Graham Bell (page 5),
Bob Bray (pages 9 and 27), John Birdsall
(page 45), Anne Crabbe (page 61),
Robert Ashby (page 77).

Cover by Martyn Chillmaid

Artwork by Norfolk House Graphic
Designers Ltd, Leicester

Printed in Great Britain by
The Alden Press Ltd, Oxford
Typeset by Typesetters (Birmingham) Ltd

The publishers wish to thank Heinemann
for permission to use material by Marie
Clay; Britt Allcroft (Thomas) Ltd for
permission to reproduce Thomas the
Tank-engine and Woodland Animations
Ltd for permission to use the illustration of
Postman Pat.

A catalogue record for this book is
available from the British Library.

ISBN 0-590-53006-2

Contents

Introduction

For children to grow up to be truly literate in a technological age, the printed word must 'speak' to them, right from babyhood, as powerfully as speech. Just as humans speak to one another to give meaning and add quality to their lives, so too must reading become valued by children as a vital lifeline to the world, enriching and informing their lives. Through reading, children can put themselves in touch with other peoples, cultures and places, the past, present and future, and with facts, fantasy, ideas, knowledge and skills. Reading is a lifeline through which they can learn to organise and take charge of their own experiences. Without reading, or when reading is confined only to functional levels, a person's life is greatly diminished.

Discovering reading

Reading should be viewed in its highest sense, as interpreting life, as in 'what do you "read into" an experience or situation?' Reading should be seen as an exciting process in which a child actively brings to it her 'self', in terms of her own ideas, thoughts, feelings, imagination and knowledge, based on her life experiences so far, and her knowledge of language, gained through talking with adults. When a child discovers something for the first time, through play, the quality of that learning experience is directly related to whether or not there is an adult with whom to share that observation. If the child is then helped to extend this experience by discovering it again in a book, in either picture or word form, then an exciting discovery has been made and the magic of books has been felt.

Throughout the process of teaching children to read and to become lifelong book-lovers, this sense of magic personal discovery must always be maintained and never rushed. It takes time to share with children their observations of the world, to help them become sensitive to their environment, and to help them verbalise what they perceive. Time thus spent is never wasted, in that books will strike an immediate chord in such children's consciousness, and will get 'under their skin' for life, as they discover part of themselves in every book they read. When books 'speak' to children in this way, it affects every aspect of their learning — for example when a child discovers for herself the magical sight of lights in houses and on roads on a dark night, then sees the images and hears the lovely poetic description of lights and moonlight in Shirley Hughes's *Lucy and Tom's ABC* (see Chapter four). This child can be encouraged to look for a variety of different kinds of light in her own world. Much later, having had her senses aroused to 'light' in this way — the feel of sunlight on a hot day on the beach, the

sight and feelings aroused by the comforting glow of the landing light — the child's creative writing may well be informed by her early first-hand and book experiences as well as her scientific awareness of different light forms, shadows, shade, and the effects of light. Books should be savoured, pictures pored over and talked about in tiny detail. Busy nursery and infant teachers are not, of course, in a position to do this as much as parents. By working closely with parents, they can ensure that the 'magic' of reading is never lost (see Chapter five). At the same time they can make sure that children develop successful reading strategies for themselves, by constantly monitoring their reading behaviour and sending home appropriate reading resources and imaginative reading games at the right 'learning moment'.

Teaching reading

In helping children to accomplish success in the reading process, the three main cuing systems of language — semantic, syntactic and graphophonic — must be constantly borne in mind by teachers, so that one is never emphasised in a child's reading programme at the expense of the others. In teaching children to read, a teacher must bear responsibility for carefully monitoring each child's development. As a result of this observation, a teacher must plan, for each child, a balanced programme of books (including 'real' and reading scheme, stories, poetry, and information), and carefully monitored approaches such as shared or paired reading, 'look and say' and phonic. Most importantly, this book advocates extremely close co-operation with parents, through the use of an informal, but none the less very important, 'reading diary' to which the child contributes as well as the parents

and teachers. This diary (see Chapter five) can be begun at the nursery stage in pictorial form, and will complement the nursery or school's own records and enable teachers to work closely with parents. With heavy curricular demands on the infant day, it is more important than ever before to maximise parental interest and help.

About this book

The ideas in this book will help nursery and infant teachers to enable children to experience reading as a satisfying, problem-solving challenge. It starts by basing children's reading experiences on highly personal experiences in the pre-school years (Chapter one); imaginative presentation of print based on the environment (Chapter two); lively book-related experiences to foster word acquisition and syntactical skills (Chapter three); and phonic development (Chapter four). The final chapter focuses on the reading diary, which charts a child's growth as a reader as he develops independent reading strategies, while always keeping hold of the 'magic'!

Reading and me

Chapter one

The relationship between listening and speaking skills and learning to read is well known. Listening to stories and talking about them is now recognised as one of the most significant factors in reading success. As well as providing a model of adult talk for vocabulary development and a basis for thinking skills, hearing stories is also important for a child's emotional growth. The telling of stories helps children to regard reading as a source of pleasure and comfort as well as a way of having their own perceptions of the world acknowledged, challenged and extended. For children to become lifelong readers, reading must enter their consciousness and 'get under their skin' in the pre-school years, ideally starting in babyhood.

The ideas in this chapter are designed to help early years teachers and parents build from the foundation of reading to children, towards ways of encouraging the children to want to become readers themselves. Children must be helped to love books so that reading 'speaks' to them as directly and powerfully as oral communication.

Literacy-based experiences in the early years must be highly personal and meaningful to a child and encourage as much speaking and listening as possible. They should enable children to come to see reading as a means of communication, both emotional and informational, between themselves and their world and between members of a family and friends, both at home and at work. The ideas will encourage children to talk about reading, especially in structured play situations. They will come to experience how reading can enhance all other aspects of their lives, whether it is wanting to find out about the world, watching television, eating, or communicating with people not actually present.

for developmental reasons or feelings of shyness in a new situation. In order to help you get to know a child as an individual and to provide you with some ideas for encouraging conversation, it can be very helpful to ask parents to fill in a 'Getting to know you' sheet. Such a sheet can prove to be an invaluable source of ideas for literacy-related activities geared to each specific child.

As a staff, brainstorm the sort of information you feel would be most useful. You could include questions about a child's favourite bedtime toy or object, her favourite kind of game or toy, television and video watching, imaginative games, any other areas of interest the child is showing curiosity about, new skills being mastered, favourite phrases, rhymes, songs, stories and types of books, names of family members, friends, pets and so on.

Getting to know you

Objective
To enable you to find out about children's home interests, in order to plan for literacy-based activities.

What you need
Photocopier or duplicator.

What to do
When a child first attends nursery or infant school, it can often take some time before she begins to talk freely, whether

Tell me about it

Objective
To encourage a child to talk about a favourite book.

What you need
A child's book from home.

What to do
Based on information gained from the 'Getting to know you' sheet (see page 10), ask a child or his parent to bring in a favourite book from home, with which the child is very familiar. Arrange a time when you can be free for a few moments to have a relaxed chat about the book, on a one-to-one basis. Research has shown (Barbara Tizard and Martin Hughes, 1984, that during such conversations, children often display complex and extended language and thinking skills, largely because they have the chance to think about the past and future. For example: 'Do you remember when you went to the beach, too?' or 'You'll be going on an aeroplane, soon, on holiday, won't you?' Initially, do not read the book to the child, but simply look at the pictures and ask the child to tell you about them. He will soon realise that you genuinely do not know what the book is about, and that you need him to explain and describe what happens. As he does so, he may relate the whole story, notice picture details for the first time and feel relaxed enough to ask you questions. In such a setting, you may find opportunities arising naturally to relate the book to the child's life, or tell anecdotes about your own childhood. By taking an interest in a child's own books in this way, you can greatly enhance his self-esteem as a reader.

A good read

Objective
For children to see teachers as role models for enjoyable reading.

What you need
Your own books from home, newspapers, magazines, children's books and so on.

What to do
This is an early years' version of USSR (uninterrupted, sustained, silent reading), an activity that is used successfully with upper infant- and junior-aged children to develop a love of silent reading. This technique involves children reading a book of their own choice, alone and silently, in the presence of their teachers, who also reads a book of his or her own, for increasing lengths of time.

With nursery- and reception-aged children, set aside a few moments on a regular basis (daily, if possible) when you tell the children that together you are going to 'settle down for a good read'. Tell the children that for a few moments they are going to be very grown-up, and look at the pictures in their books and 'read in their head', just like you! The children may bring in their favourite books from home, if they wish.

At the start of the session, let each child choose, say, three or four books, or for children who are new to this activity, enough to keep them going for just one minute. You will find that, over a period of time, even nursery-aged children will sit for longer and longer as they become immersed in their books.

It is very important for the impact of this activity, that the books you read are genuinely your own books from home, and not the children's books. Bring in a novel, factual book, newspaper or magazine. After a moment or two of you and the children all 'reading' silently to yourselves, warn the children that the session is nearly at an end. Then close your book and tell the children all about your 'good read'. Next, let the children tell you about theirs.

Talk about, or show them, if possible, books you loved as a child, not forgetting to mention the exciting fact that you perhaps read some of them in bed at night, by torchlight! Occasionally, bring in a book from which you can take notes, such as a cookery book, or a travel brochure. Make the notes as you read, and then show the children what you have written.

My favourite video

Objective
To help a child associate the pleasure of television and video viewing with the pleasure of reading.

What you need
Television, video-recorder, children's favourite video films, television magazines, comics, related books, paper, crayons, pens, stapler, paintings, model and puppet-making materials.

What to do
Many children have a favourite television programme or video film which has been bought for them. These can be very

important to a child and, in the case of videos, can often be played again and again by the child, becoming like a favourite book.

As a starting point, it is useful to regard children's interest in television in the same way as if it were an interest in books. Talk to individual children about their favourite programmes and films and try to develop the interest into all areas of the curriculum, with reading as an integral part of every stage.

Often, the visual impact of television is so strong that children can appear to sit passively, not interacting with the programme or using their imaginative and thinking skills as they would with a book. However, as with books, if adults have knowledge of the content of the programmes and films, and the time to discuss them with children individually, then television watching can become a motivating catalyst for children to become readers and active meaning-makers and problem-solvers, in different areas of their lives.

Ask a child about her favourite programme or video, watch it yourself, or ask the child's parents if you may borrow the video for an evening. The following day, talk to the child about it, helping her to recall events, verbalise the plot and give an opinion about the characters' personalities and actions. If possible, talk to the parents about what you are doing so that they, too, can try talking with their children in this way.

After having this sort of discussion with the children, there are many reading-related activities possible, all of which are, of course, suitable for developing an interest arising from a book, as well as from a programme or video. For example:

● Write a story together, and make it into a book for shared reading — either a literal or an imaginative version of the programme or video.

● Ask the child to draw the main characters. You, or the child, can write their names underneath, for the child to read. Cut out pictures and/or printed names from television magazines and comics, for added visual impact.
● Draw the characters, or cut them from comics, and draw speech bubbles next to them, containing their most famous expressions, for the child to read.
● Make simple puppets, and agree on what each will say in a show. Give each child a very short, simple script written in large letters.
● Write down the words of any theme song, or song on a related theme.
● Provide theme sets and play people for 'storying' (see page 16), for example, a train set to recreate a 'Thomas the Tank-engine' video story.

- Help the children to make up rhymes or riddles about the characters, write them down, and let the children read them out loud to each other.
- Let the children and staff mime or act out roles from the programmes or films. Other children must ask questions, to find out who is being represented.
- Let the children paint pictures and make models of the characters and where they live. Where appropriate, in model making, write out very simple step-by-step instructions for the children to read and follow.
- Find 'books of the film' and story or information books on similar themes, to read to or with a child, for example, books about real turtles, ponies, bears and so on. Some children may then wish to make their own scrap books or project books containing, for example, information on the many different breeds of ponies or bears.
- Play part of a child's favourite video to the rest of the children. Ask them what they think has happened before the extract and what will happen next. BBC videos are especially suitable, for example, Thomas the Tank-engine, Fireman Sam and Postman Pat.

Bedtime story

Objective

To encourage a love of stories through role-play and role-reversal.

What you need

A child's favourite book, favourite teddy or doll, home corner furniture, bean-bag, blanket.

What to do

Send a letter home to one or several children's parents, asking if the children could bring in a current favourite book, or a book from babyhood, and a teddy or doll. Play 'bedtime story', in which the child pretends to be the 'parent', tucking up teddy in the home corner and 'reading' a favourite story.

An enjoyable variation of this activity is for an adult to assume the role of a child going to bed, curling up on, say, a bean-bag, complete with blanket, while the child, as the parent, 'reads' a story.

It may be possible for a parent or member of staff to bring in a favourite book from their childhood, and talk about how their parents read it to them.

Weekend world

Objectives
To enable children to recall events, discuss them and translate them into book form.

What you need
Photocopier or duplicator, paper, crayons, pen, hole punch, ribbon or string.

What to do
Occasionally, send a letter home asking parents to fill in a very simple 'diary', consisting of three things their children did on either a Saturday or Sunday; for example, one thing for the morning, afternoon and early evening. Explain that this information is going to be used to make a personalised book for their child, and that the activities need not be anything special or unusual.

When the diaries have been returned to you, discuss them with each child, and make a very simple book together based on the information. If possible, let the child draw each activity on a separate piece of paper, and dictate a caption to you, or you can draw the pictures. Mix up the pictures and see whether the child can lay them in the correct sequence. Let the child then decorate a cover for the book, entitled 'My Saturday (Sunday)

book'. Punch two holes on the left-hand side of each piece of paper, and help the child to thread ribbon or string through the holes to secure the pages. Finally, you can help the child to read the book, using shared reading.

Just the book for you!

Objective
To match a book with a child's particular interest or current experience.

What you need
Wide variety of story and information books.

What to do
An obvious, but highly effective way of helping children to become lifelong readers, is to let them borrow a book which closely relates to their current interests. For this to have maximum impact, you need to know the child's home pursuits and experiences, for example, from the 'Getting to know you' sheet (see page 10), or a 'Weekend world' diary (see page 15). In the case of the latter, the information that the family had a day trip to the seaside could, for example, give rise to the child's taking home a copy of *Bears Who Went to the Seaside* by Suzanna Gretz. Similarly, for the child whose 'getting to know you' sheet indicates that he is trying very hard to dress himself, *How Do I Put It On?* by Shigeo Watanabe is just the book!

Children, and parents, very much appreciate it when staff can match books in this personal and timely way.

Books, books everywhere!

Objective

To familiarise children with the wide variety of book forms available.

What you need

Photograph albums, pattern books, diaries, DIY books, encyclopaedias, 'novelty' books and so on.

What to do

Display a wide range of different types of book, to show children how the book format is used in different spheres of life. Make sure that you change the display regularly and include some of the following:

• collections and albums, for example, photographs, stamps, football stickers, pressed flowers, fruit stickers, postcards and so on;
• books which help us to choose objects, patterns and designs, for example, wallpaper pattern books, fabric swatches, carpet samples, merchandise catalogues (especially toys), seed catalogues and so on;
• books which show us how to do things, for example, cookery books, DIY manuals, car manuals, and so on;
• books which help us to find people and places, for example, telephone directories, A-Zs, atlases and so on;
• handwritten books, for example, diaries, students' ring files, nursery/school registers, children's project books (from infant and junior schools) and so on;
• boxed sets of books and books with interesting bindings, for example, encyclopaedias, bibles, leather-bound volumes and so on;
• novelty books, pop-up books, big books, concertina and fabric books. The children could make some very simple versions of these, especially concertina books.

Storying

Objective

To help children develop imaginative story-telling skills.

What you need

Wide variety of story-books, miniature play people and 'theme' sets, construction toys, such as DUPLO, empty food containers and so on.

What to do

Find out from a child, and/or the 'Weekend world' diaries (see page 15), about an outing she may have been on recently. Let her tell you about it and possibly act out some of the events. If possible, at this stage, try and find a related story book. After reading the book and discussing it, let the child further recreate her experience, through 'storying'. Provide her with play people, 'theme sets', construction sets and/or empty food containers, and let her re-enact her experience in miniature. Stay unobtrusively close by, and try and jot down, if possible, some of her phrases as she talks through her story, which by this time will incorporate elements of her real-life experience, combined with words and ideas from the story you have read together.

After 'storying', some children may like to dictate the story to you, to make a book of their own.

An example of the 'storying' technique could be the child who goes on a boat trip, reads *Meg At Sea* by Helen Nicoll and Jan Pienkowski, and builds a DUPLO boat for a DUPLO bear who gets shipwrecked and rescued by a helicopter. This could then form the basis for the child's book about the shipwrecked bear.

I've done that!

Objective
For children to learn to empathise with story characters.

What you need
Story-books.

What to do
It is customary for children to mime or act out a story in their role-play after hearing it read to them. However, for a change try the reverse process. Have a story in mind, for example *Whatever Next!* by Jill Murphy and, one morning, show the children a large cardboard box. Tell them that it is a space rocket and that they are going to fly to the moon in it! Ask them what they think they would see on the way. Let the children sit on the floor in their imaginary rockets and pretend to be flying to the moon. Accept all their ideas, and add the ideas from the story, such as meeting the owl, waving to an aeroplane, landing on the moon, having a picnic and getting rained on.

In the afternoon of the same day, or possibly the following day, with no preamble, read the story from the book, and enjoy the looks of delighted recognition on the children's faces, as the connection between their imaginary game and the story dawns on them!

Rhyme time

Objective

For children to relate emotionally-significant aural and oral experiences (such as nursery rhymes and songs) to the printed word.

What you need

Card, paper, felt-tipped pens, plastic wallets or clear self-adhesive plastic, rhyme anthologies.

What to do

From babyhood, children enjoy the experience of being cuddled while listening to nursery rhymes and songs. In time, these become a very important part of children's early language, in that they signify to them emotional security and the pleasures of communication. Capture the delight children take in saying and singing rhymes, and transpose this to a reading context by simply writing out the words of a child's favourite rhyme or songs on card, and adding a few simple illustrations of your own. Put the card in a plastic wallet, or cover it with film, and let the child 'read' the words using shared reading (or singing!).

Let the child borrow the card to take home. Because he will already be familiar with the words, rhyme, rhythm and repetition, the child will find to his delight that he can 'read' the card virtually instantly. These cards can be a highly motivating way of encouraging early reading.

Many children make up their own songs. Write down these words on card, too. Have available a selection of rhyme anthologies, so you can always be ready to introduce new rhymes to individual children in order to acknowledge and extend a current interest. *This Little Puffin* (ed. E. Matterson), for example, contains a comprehensive collection of rhymes and songs on a very wide range of subjects. A child who is interested in elephants, for example, could draw one on the front of a folded card, with the words of one of the elephant rhymes from *This Little Puffin* written inside, for him to read.

Baby albums

Objective

For children to see parents and staff communicating with each other about the children's past lives, through the written word of the baby album.

What you need

Baby albums or books, *Baby's Catalogue* (Janet and Allan Ahlberg), paper, crayon, pens, hole punch, ribbon or string.

What to do

Ask the children or their parents to bring in their baby albums or books. Read any captions written by the parents, with the child, asking questions in order to amplify the details.

Make a simple book called 'I grow up' along the same lines as the 'Weekend world' book (see page 15). Discuss suitable captions with the child, for example: 'At first I could only lie down. Then I sat up. Then I crawled'. Let the child draw the pictures, and see if she can sequence the pages correctly, before tying them together using ribbon or string tied through holes made with a hole punch.

Birthday book

Objective

For children to share written communication from relatives and friends, with you.

What you need

A child's birthday cards, hole punch, ribbon or string, sugar paper, felt-tipped pen.

What to do

When a child has a birthday ask a parent if he or she would like to send in some or all of the child's birthday cards, about a week after receiving them. These can then be assembled into a birthday book for the child to take home and keep.

When the child brings in the cards, help him to punch two holes on the left-hand side of each card. (With thick cards, it may be necessary to use an awl.) The child can then enjoy threading ribbon or string through the cards to hold them all together.

Read through the messages on the cards with the child, and have a chat about them. Finally, help the child to make a cover out of sugar paper and write 'My birthday book' on the front. On the inside of the cover write 'These people sent me cards . . .', and help the child to tell you who sent each card, and write down their names in the same order as the cards appear in the book. If you wish, you can help the child to put numbers at the bottom of the cards like page numbers (four numbers to each card), and then add a number next to each name on the inside cover, to encourage number recognition.

In the news

Objective

For children to enjoy the pleasure of communicating information about themselves through the written word.

What you need

Photocopier, borrowed photograph of each child, local newspapers, card, felt-tipped pen, plastic wallets, easel, sugar paper, bulldog clip.

What to do

Ask parents to lend you a photograph of their child for the day. Preferably the photograph should show the child involved in some activity, either alone or with others. Photocopy the photograph, so that it appears at the top of an A4 sheet of paper. (It is a good idea to make several copies as they are very useful.) Discuss with the child what is happening in the picture, and explain that you are going to write this down so that other people may read it, as they would in a newspaper. Show the children some copies of a local newspaper and point out articles, announcements and so on. Agree with the child what you are going to write, and think of a headline. At the top of each sheet, write information for parents, for example: 'Please read to me, or with me, using shared reading'. When you have written the sheet, stick it on to a piece of card, and slip it into a plastic wallet.

The children will greatly enjoy taking home cards about their friends, and trying to read all about them to their parents. They are also very thrilled when their own card is chosen by another child to take home.

Make larger versions of these news cards. If you hear of family news, such as the birth of a baby, write about it on a large sheet of paper, and attach it to an easel, so that it can be read with all the children.

Name games

Objective

For a child to recognise her own first and second names.

What you need

Photocopier, borrowed photograph of each child, card, felt-tipped pen, clear self-adhesive film.

What to do

A child's name is, of course, tremendously important to her, and a very powerful incentive for reading. Make name cards, including surnames, for all the children, and a set of photocopied photographs,

stuck on to card and covered in clear self-adhesive plastic. Many games can then be devised using the name cards and photographs, for example:
● At milk time, place a name card and/ or photograph card at each place, for the children to find their seat and/or to put their name and photograph together.
● Occasionally put all the cards with a first name beginning with the same letter together, and see whether the children realise what they all have in common. On another day, do the same with surnames.
● Write the children's first and second names on paper, and cut them so that the names are separated. Put several names on a table for a child to pair up the first and second names correctly. It is fun, too, to let the children interchange each other's first and surnames deliberately!

Poorly Postman Pat

Objectives
For children to appreciate the significance of communicating by letter, and to learn to read their own addresses.

What you need
Paper, envelopes, stamps, pens, Postman Pat doll, photocopier, empty powder-paint drum, red paper, cardboard carton, photocopiable page 88.

What to do
Send a copy of the letter on photocopiable page 88 through the post to each child's house. To help with the cost of the stamps, write out the following message, and hand it to each parent about a week before you intend to send the letters: 'Next week, we would like to send your child a real letter through the post, from Postman Pat. (Please keep this a secret from your child!) To help defray the cost of postage, we would very much appreciate it if you could please put the cost of a first class stamp into this box. Thank you very much'.

Once the children have all received their letters encourage them to write their own letters or make cards for Postman Pat, using their own level of emergent writing. Let them post them in a home-made letter-box made by covering an empty powder-paint drum with red paper, having first cut out a slit for the letters. The next day have ready either a giant letter from Postman Pat to thank everybody, or individual letters 'delivered', this time, to the nursery or school.

Follow-up
Write each child's name and address on an empty envelope and draw a picture of a stamp on it. Flatten a box and draw a door shape on it. Cut out the door and cut a hole for the letters in it. Let each child pretend to be Postman Pat, with a bag containing, say, three envelopes, out of which he must recognise his own, and post it through the letter-box in the cardboard door.

21

Shopping by book

Objective
For children to become familiar with the idea of using a book (catalogue) to facilitate shopping.

What you need
Catalogue shop catalogues, mail-order and educational suppliers' catalogues, 'copy-safe' plastic wallets, ribbon or string, scissors, A4 white paper, adhesive, felt-tipped pens, toy money, old cheque book covers, stapler, cardboard carton, postman or woman's outfit, photocopier.

What to do
Children love to pore over the toy pages in the catalogues of catalogue shops and mail-order companies. Capitalise on this by turning this interest into a literary-based activity, involving reading, emergent writing and structured play.

Cut out about six pictures of toys, for which you have an identical, or very similiar, real object, for example, a bike, a doll, a teddy, a DUPLO box, a brand name toy and a jigsaw. Stick two pictures on an A4 sheet, and write the name of the toy and a price, in pounds only, beneath each picture. Slip each sheet into a plastic wallet, and secure it with a ribbon. Make a simple cover, and the catalogue is complete.

Set up a catalogue shop, where each child chooses a toy, fills in an order form (simply designed and photocopied by you), gives it to the shopkeeper with the money, and then receives the toy.

Alternatively, use the catalogue for shopping by post. This way a child chooses a toy, fills in a form and pretends to post it. A post person can then collect the forms, and take them to the 'toy warehouse'. The warehouse person can then put the toys in a carton, 'write' the address and give them to the postman or woman to deliver.

Group stories

Objectives

To heighten children's awareness of their environment through sensory exploration, and for them to verbalise this and see their observations written down, for others to read.

What you need

A variety of interesting objects, natural and man-made; large and small sheets of paper, felt-tipped pens, plastic wallets.

What to do

As part of children's scientific awareness, give them regular access to interesting objects. Help and encourage them to describe the objects using all their senses. Create a group story by writing down their comments either on large sheets of paper to form part of wall displays of the children's paintings and collages, or on small sheets, which can be put inside plastic wallets and borrowed for home

reading. A full description of how to produce 'group stories' can be found in *Young Children in Action*, by Mary Hohmann, Bernard Banet and David P. Weikart (High/Scope Press).

Children are usually very pleased to have their perceptions of the world, and those of their friends, acknowledged in this way.

Follow-up

After some practice with group stories in verbalising descriptions, children can become quite proficient at making up riddles. They will be able to look at an object hidden from the sight of the others and describe it to them so that they can guess what it is; for example, 'It is red and round. It has skin and a stalk. You can eat it. What is it?'

Book talk

Objective

To encourage children to talk about books through structured play situations.

What you need

Well-known children's books, empty chocolate boxes, white paper, adhesive, felt-tipped pens, cards, scissors, Blu-Tack, toy money, DUPLO.

What to do

From time to time, transform the home corner into a book shop, library or video shop. Cover empty chocolate boxes with white paper and decorate them with the titles and pictures of books or films, selecting titles with which the children are very familiar. Let the children interchange roles as customers, shopkeepers, borrowers and librarians. Much dialogue can ensue about the kinds of books available, plots, recommendations and so on.

Stick temporary price labels on the books with Blu-Tack, for the book shop, and use DUPLO to make a pretend date stamp for the library.

What a lovely book!

Objectives
For children to perceive books as an attractive gift, and to familiarise them with the pleasure of giving and receiving books as presents.

What you need
Children's books, card, felt-tipped pens, Blu-Tack, toy money, soft toys, wrapping paper, pencils, writing paper, scissors.

What to do
Set up a mini-bookshop, as in the previous activity, and attach prices to each book using Blu-Tack. Choose only about five books, for which you have a related soft toy, such as a Postman Pat book, a teddy bear book, a rabbit book, a duck book, a panda book and so on. Arrange the soft toys on a table, and the books, upright, on another table. Tell the children that it is the birthday of each of the soft toys and that they would all love to have a book for a present. Each child should then choose a toy for whom he wishes to buy a book and decide which book he thinks the toy would like. It needn't, of course, necessarily be the one about the toy!

When the child has chosen a book, he can pay the correct amount of toy money to the bookshop keeper, who can wrap up the book. (Use Blu-Tack so that the paper may be reused). Help the child to write the name of the recipient on a small piece of paper and to stick it on the wrapping paper with Blu-Tack. The child can then give the book to the soft toy. Use your skill as a ventriloquist to enable the toy to say 'thank you'!

Follow-up

Ask each child to choose a book he thinks a friend would like. Again, help him wrap the book, and label it. Children do readily accept that they cannot, of course, keep these books!

place and then be returned. When cool the models can be painted with powder paints and varnished when dry. Add any further props and dressing-up clothes as appropriate and let the children pretend to be the customers, waiters, waitresses, shopkeepers and so on. Emphasise the importance of reading the menu, and writing out the order and bill.

What shall I have?

Objectives

For children to experience reading names of favourite foods from a menu and ordering them.

What you need

Large sheet of white paper, felt-tipped pens, salt pastry (3 cups of plain flour, 2 cups of salt, 4 teaspoons of wallpaper paste powder [without fungicide], 1⅓ cups of water all mixed together), magazine pictures of food, cardboard, clear self-adhesive plastic, scissors, table cloths, crockery, note pads, pens, toy money, dressing-up clothes.

What to do

Discuss with the children their favourite foods. Write them down on a large piece of paper and let the children illustrate them. Stick the menu on the wall. Arrange the home corner either as a café/fast food restaurant or as a take-away shop. Let the children make models of the food from salt pastry, or cut out magazine pictures and stick them on cardboard and cover them with self-adhesive plastic. Bake the dough shapes in a very cold oven (70°C or gas mark ½) for a minimum of 12 hours. If necessary they can be taken out of the oven to allow normal cooking to take

Let me write that down

Objective

For children to appreciate the importance of writing and reading in communicating urgent information.

What you need

Toy telephones, message pads, pencils, toy cars and ambulance, road mats, toy microphone, play people, model village buildings.

What to do

Arrange various play situations in which a child listens to a telephone message and has to 'write' it down, and 'read' it to a third party. There are many possibilities for such situations, for example:

● An amusing telephone message to the nursery or school; for example, a new little girl called Mary will be arriving soon, but her lamb is following her. Can someone arrange to look after the lamb? The child must 'write' this message down on the message pad, and tell a teacher about it. Arrange for Mary and lamb to arrive!

● When children are playing with cars on the carpet, set up a motor breakdown service office, where a child can sit and receive telephone messages from stranded motorists, who must give their location. The telephonist must then relay the location to a patrol person through a radio microphone.

● Similarly, using toy cars, play people, a toy ambulance and model village buildings, set up an emergency exchange, where the operator must write down details of car accidents, fires, lost items and so on. These details will have to be 'read' to the hospital, fire station or police.

● Let the children take turns pretending to be a doctor's receptionist, 'writing' down a message about a sick patient (symptoms, address and so on). The receptionist must then 'read' these details to the 'doctor'.

Print world

Chapter two

As a child's vision of the world begins to widen from home and family to the world outside, literacy-based experiences should be broadened to emphasise environmental print in all its forms. Pre-school children delight in gradually becoming more independent of their parents and are proud to show off their new 'reading' skills in recognising words in different situations throughout the day — at home, on journeys, while shopping and at school. Children feel very grown up when they can recognise logos, advertisements and signs, and when they can play a part in searching for information, be it their favourite programme in a television magazine or the destination printed on the number 42 bus.

Road reading

Objective

To encourage awareness of road traffic signs.

What you need

A copy of *The Highway Code*, scissors, two sets of miniature road signs, movable rounders posts, card, chalk, red, yellow, green and black sugar paper, paper-clips.

What to do

Show the children a copy of *The Highway Code* and explain that grown-ups have to learn all the road signs before they can pass their driving test and that it is safer also for cyclists to know all the signs before cycling in busy traffic. After playing matching games and snap with mounted road signs, send a letter home asking parents to bring in their child's tricycle or bike for a specific road safety day.

Draw out some road signs on thick card and attach them to rounders posts. Chalk out a roadway complete with pedestrian crossing on the school playground. Let the children take turns to be the police directing the traffic. You could also have a group of children pretending to be workmen digging up the road, placing a 'Stop when the light is on red' sign nearby. You could add a 'Go when the light is on green' sign and use circles of coloured sugar paper stuck on to a rectangular piece of black card for the lights. Change the lights by covering up the circles with black paper attached with paper-clips.

You can then ask groups of children to ride slowly along the roadways taking note of and following the instructions on all the road signs, both those with symbols and those with writing.

Follow that sign

Objective
To encourage the ability to follow simple written instructions.

What you need
Paper, felt-tipped pens, Blu-Tack.

What to do
Compile a series of instruction cards which can be stuck on the classroom door so that the children see them as they come in from outdoor play. The cards can be decorated with picture clues and should contain such instructions as: 'Go and wash your hands', or 'Go and sit at the art table'.

Different instructions could be given to different groups of children, possibly on colour-coded paper or using a group symbol in the corner of the card.

Please fasten your seat-belts

Objective
To encourage an awareness of print in the environment.

What you need
Belts, card, felt-tipped pens, atlas.

What to do
This activity is particularly appropriate near the summer holiday break when some children will be flying abroad. Use the structured play area to set up an aeroplane scene. Use all the signs that might actually be found on board an aeroplane, including 'No smoking', 'Exit' and so on. Set out chairs in two rows and drape belts over them, so that the children can pretend to fasten their seat-belts.

Look at an atlas together to decide on a suitable destination!

Follow-up
The children might also have fun making up a suitable menu for an in-flight meal.

Let me read you

Objective
To make children aware that words are all around them including on clothing.

What you need
Fabric crayons, duplicating paper, photocopier.

What to do
Nowadays many items of clothing, both adult and children's, incorporate words and captions as part of their design. Send a letter to the children's parents informing them of a special school day when the children should try to wear an item of clothing with writing on it, such as a slogan or simply the name of the designer prominently displayed. On the day encourage the children to 'read' each other's clothes.

Follow-up
The children could be asked to bring in a plain white T-shirt which they could then decorate with their own pictures and captions (dictated to the teacher) using fabric crayons.

Signs, signs everywhere

Objective
To heighten awareness of signs in the environment.

What you need
Card, felt-tipped pens.

What to do
Put up lots of signs around the classroom that the children are likely to see when they are out with their parents. For example, draw a simple logo illustrating someone putting litter in the bin and write the words 'Put your litter in here' and draw an arrow. Label the classroom door 'Entrance' and 'Exit'. Draw simple signs for the toilets with the words 'Boys' and 'Girls' on them, and write 'Now wash your hands please' above a picture of a pair of hands under a running tap.

Do not feed the animals

Objective

To encourage awareness of a wide variety of signs when going on favourite outings.

What you need

Miniature zoo animals, coloured sugar paper, foil, felt-tipped pens, card, miniature play figures, small bricks.

What to do

Almost all children enjoy going to the zoo and looking at all the animals. Develop an awareness of environmental print at the zoo by setting out a miniature zoo in the classroom. Use coloured sugar paper as a base and add foil for the water for the penguins, sea lions and so on. Make brick boundaries for the different varieties of animal and place in each enclosure a small sign giving the animal's country of origin, for example, 'Elsa the elephant comes from Africa'.

Ask the children to pretend that the family of miniature play figures have never been to a zoo before and might get lost. Can the children help to make lots of signs to help the family find their way around? These might include signs saying: 'This way to the reptile house', 'Please keep off the grass', 'Do not feed the animals' and 'The dolphin show starts at 2 o'clock'.

The children could then 'walk' the miniature figures round the zoo reading all the signs as they go.

Commercial break

Objective

For children to be able to 'read' adverts in television, magazines and newspapers.

What you need

Large cardboard box, Blu-Tack, magazine adverts, felt-tipped pens, sugar paper, paints, card.

What to do

Make a television out of a large cardboard box by cutting out a square for the screen, painting or covering it with sugar paper and drawing the dials with a felt-tipped pen. Cut out a variety of well-known adverts from magazines and stick them with Blu-Tack one at a time on to the television screen. Do the children recognise the adverts by the picture alone, or do they use the written word as a clue to its identity? Read through the adverts with the children.

Follow-up

Play a form of lotto by giving each of three children a large card containing four adverts. When an advert appears on the television screen and on their card they can place a counter on the relevant picture on their card. The winner is the child to have covered all her pictures with counters.

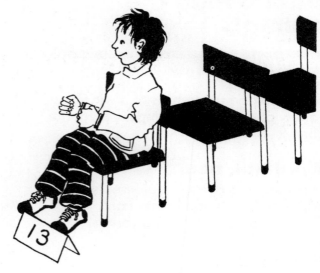

Where to?

Objective

For children to be able to recognise the names of local areas in a role-play situation.

What you need

Cereal boxes, card, felt-tipped pens, pennies, shoulder bag, sticky labels, road mat.

What to do

Turn the home corner into a bus station for the day by positioning nine chairs in rows of three, one behind the other to make three buses. Attach a sign to each 'bus', possibly with Blu-Tack, giving the number of the bus and its destination, based on different areas where the children might live.

A group of children can take turns to decide where they would like to go and which number bus they need to board. The driver on each bus should decide how much the passengers need to pay (between 1p and 5p) and after handing over the correct change they can climb aboard. When one bus is full with two passengers the rest of the children will have to choose another destination.

The bus station scene can also be enacted using decorated cereal boxes as bus models, play people as passengers and a road mat. Use sticky labels to write the destination and number on each bus and to label the street names on the road mat.

Out and about

Objective
For children to be able to identify signs in the local environment.

What you need
Duplicating paper, photocopier.

What to do
Take the children on a short walk, but before you take them walk round the route by yourself, making a note of any signs that the children might notice as they go past, for example, 'Beware of the dog' on a gate, 'Litter' on a litter bin, 'Footpath' on a small sign and so on. Draw about six of these signs on a piece of duplicating paper. Draw the outline of the sign so that it provides a clue to the meaning of the sign. For example, draw a dog for the sign: 'Beware of the dog'.

Display an enlarged version of the sheet in the classroom a few days before you take the children on the walk to encourage group discussion and to give the children a chance to look out for the signs on their way home.

On the day of the walk, give each child a pencil and a sheet of signs so that they can circle each sign as they see them.

A simpler version of this activity would be to explore the immediate environment within the nursery or school, looking for instructional labels, such as on/off, push/pull, emergency exit and so on.

Shop and read

Objective

For children to be able to identify both well-known and local shop logos.

What you need

Small cartons, large cardboard boxes, boxes and bags from different shops displaying the shop logo, two-minute egg timer.

What to do

Turn three large boxes into models of well-known shops by cutting out large windows and doors from the front of the box. Label each box with a logo cut from a high-street store's carrier bag. Collect bags or cartons from these well-known shops ensuring that each bag or carton displays the shop logo. Make a pile of these bags in the middle of the table and ask individual, pairs or small groups of children to try to sort the bags and cartons into the different shops in two minutes.

NB Never let children play with plastic bags without an adult present.

Follow-up

If the children all live within the same area, make a collection of paper and plastic bags from local shops and compare their logos. Sort out objects that might be bought from one of these shops, such as a cake from the bakers' shop, a piece of fruit from the grocers and so on. Can the children put the objects in the correct bags?

Going up

Objective

To help the children become aware of environmental print in large department stores.

What you need

Paper, felt-tipped pens, sticky labels, scissors, catalogues, magazines, official-looking cap.

What to do

One of the main attractions for small children of going shopping in a big department store is using the lift to go up to different floors. Develop this interest by making a pretend lift, possibly using the entrance to the home corner. Encourage the children to decide which floor they wish to go up to by making a large sign numbered one to five and labelled with the wares displayed on each floor. The children can help make this sign by cutting out relevant pictures from magazines and catalogues to stick next to the appropriate wording.

The lift boy or girl, wearing an official-looking cap, can ask the customer which floor she would like to go up to and press the numbered sticky labels to make the lift 'move'.

Alternatively, the customer might ask the lift boy or girl where various articles of clothing or household goods might be found.

Explain to the children that real lifts can only bear so much weight, and put up a sign determining the maximum number of children allowed in the classroom lift. Perhaps take the opportunity to warn them that they should never play in or near lifts because of the dangers of trapping their fingers in the lift doors.

Which car?

Objectives
To encourage children to look for writing on vehicles and be able to distinguish between different makes of car.

What you need
Car brochures and magazines, card, felt-tipped pen, Playmobil people.

What to do
Take the children into the staff car park and discuss the features on different makes of car. Point out that the make of each car is usually written on the back or front of the vehicle.

When you return to the classroom, let the children look through the brochures and magazines. Can they match toy cars to the pictures in the brochures? As the children identify each toy car, write the car's make on a label and stand it next to the car. Let the children use Playmobil figures to act out the scene of a person coming to a car showroom to buy a new car. The salesperson should point out the different models in the showroom, reading the labels as he performs the sales pitch.

Follow-up
Jumble up the name labels for about five cars and see if pairs of children can match them up to the correct car. Use names that have different initial letters.

Read and choose

Objectives
For children to recognise brand labels on toy boxes, toy adverts and toy catalogues and put this knowledge to use.

What you need
Toy brand name labels, toy catalogues, simplified requisition sheet, card, clear self-adhesive plastic.

What to do
Involve the children in the task of ordering new equipment and toys for the classroom. Ask their opinions about what new toys would be useful or which construction games need new pieces. Familiarise the children with the toy

brand names by cutting out and mounting name labels from toy boxes and old catalogues. Cover these with clear self-adhesive plastic.

Display four or five of these different toys. Can the children match the labels to the toys? Continue to do this for about a week, changing the toys every day, so that the children become familiar with a wide variety of common toy brands.

At the beginning of the following week, sit with a group of children as they browse through toy catalogues making their personal choices for the classroom. They will enjoy recognising the brand names of their favourite toys. Explain to the children that some of the toys they choose might have to be ordered the next year when more money has been saved up, but let them see pictures of their final choices.

When the toys arrive, ask the children to read the labels on the boxes and tick off the order on a simplified requisition sheet (complete with pictures clues).

Read and snack

Objective
To be able to recognise the writing on favourite chocolate and biscuit bars.

What you need
Chocolate bar or biscuit wrappers, card, adhesive.

What to do
Send a letter to parents asking them to save the wrappers from any biscuit or chocolate bars eaten by the children over the next two weeks. These can, of course, include healthier snack bars with a low sugar content! Specify in the letter a day on which all the children should bring their wrappers into nursery or school.

Help the children to stick their wrappers on to a piece of card, and let them spend time discussing their favourite chocolate and biscuit bars. Can they spot their favourite bar on a friend's card?

Choose a card containing about four wrappers and play an I-spy game using the first sound.

Follow-up

Ask the children, in turn, to come to the front of the class and describe their favourite bar without saying its name, for example: 'My favourite bar has lots of little holes in it, and has a brown or green wrapper'. Can the other children guess what it is?

Alternatively, make models of bars of chocolate using salt dough (see page 25) and stick the wrappers round them. Use these models in a classroom shop. The children can then choose the bar they want from a large card display of different wrappers.

What's on?

Objective

To encourage children to recognise the titles of favourite television programmes.

What you need

Duplicating paper, photocopier, photocopiable page 89.

What to do

Send a letter to parents asking them to look through a television magazine with their children and cut out the caption announcing the title and time of their favourite television programme. Provide a tear-off section at the bottom of the

letter where the television title can be stuck and returned to school.

After group discussion about the programme content, each child can draw a scene on the television screen on photocopiable page 89 and you can write the title underneath.

Encourage the children to discuss exactly when they watch their favourite programme — it might be when they get in from school while they have a drink and a biscuit and before a parent comes home from work.

Display the sheets randomly at eye level where the children can look to see who else likes the same programme as they do. This will involve the children in matching the titles of the programmes. Can they count to see which is the most popular programme?

Sort it out

Objective
To aid word recognition in a practical sorting context.

What you need
Plastic baskets, paper, felt-tipped pen, sticky labels, duplicating paper, photocopier.

What to do
Sort the school lost property box into different plastic baskets which have been labelled: jumpers, hats, scarves, toys and so on. This will mean that when the children are looking for a lost possession in future they will be reading the labels at the same time.

Occasionally make a game out of sorting the lost property by piling it all together and asking pairs of children to put the items in the correct baskets.

Follow-up
Use this activity in an imaginative play situation with a dolls' or teddies' lost property box.

Neat and tidy

Objective

To use word recognition as a means to help classroom organisation.

What you need

Felt-tipped pen, sticky labels, duplicating paper, photocopier, dressing-up items, dolls' clothes, containers, hooks.

What to do

Prevent the dressing-up box from getting into a tangle by having separate hooks or containers for each type of clothing.

Label these clearly, perhaps using shelves to hold hats, bags, purses and so on. Help the children to practise replacing the items they have used in the correct place by initially using sticky tape to attach a label to the item itself. This way the children can match them with the label on the shelf or container. Dolls' clothes can also be sorted into different labelled containers.

Follow-up

Give each child three sticky labels to take home with them. These labels should list three different items of clothing, for example, socks, vests and pants. In a covering letter ask parents to attach these labels to clothes drawers. This will help the children with both word recognition and independent dressing.

The ice-cream van's coming

Objective

To encourage the children to look closely at the names of their favourite ice lollies.

What you need

Duplicating paper, photocopier, stiff card, scissors, paint, felt-tipped pens, stick tape or adhesive, white shirt, tape recorder, percussion instruments.

What to do

Send a letter home asking the children and parents to save ice lolly wrappers and washed lolly sticks. Set a day for them to be brought into school for sorting into matching pairs. (One of the wrappers in the pair will be displayed on a menu board while the other will be made into a model lolly and sold from the van.)

Cut, stick and paint large sheets of stiff card so that they resemble the basic shape of an ice-cream van and attach them to a table or free standing shelving unit. Make sure that you leave a window in the van through which the model ice

lollies can be served. Help the children to make a lollipop menu board by sticking the real wrappers on to it and printing the lolly names under each one. The children can make model ice lollies by stuffing the wrappers with scrunched up paper and sticking them to real lolly sticks. They can then take turns to point to the lolly of their choice on the menu board and read its name. The ice-cream man or woman, wearing a cut down adult white shirt as an overall, can serve the children with the correct lolly.

Follow-up

Have fun recording a made up ice-cream jingle on tape using classroom percussion instruments and remind the children that they must never run into the road to get to an ice-cream van quickly. The classroom 'van' might display a road safety warning on its side, illustrated by the children.

Read and shop

Objective

To encourage familiarity with common food labels.

What you need

Labels from tinned food, card, clear self-adhesive plastic.

What to do

Collect matching pairs of labels from food tins. Mount each one on card and cover with protective film. These cards can then be used for sorting activities, both into cards that are identical (snap

41

games) and those that have the same sort of wording, for example, the '57 varieties' tins. Most children are very quick to 'read' the labels on tins as the writing is often so distinctive and there are added colour and picture clues.

Set up food tins in the structured play area for a shopping session. The children can use the food label cards to help them write out a shopping list.

NB Never leave children playing with food tins without adult supervision, as they could drop the tins on their toes.

Follow-up

If possible, take groups of children to a supermarket on a quiet day to shop for ingredients for a class meal. How many of the packages do they recognise? Discuss what sort of items are grouped together.

Breakfast reading

Objective

To recognise the names of common breakfast cereals.

What you need

Two variety packs of cereals, large empty cereal boxes, bowls, spoons.

What to do

Set up a breakfast bar in the structured play area, pouring out a small amount of cereal from each box of a variety pack. Jumble up the boxes and see if the children can match the boxes to the bowl of cereal by looking at the picture. Let them have a taste of each cereal. Which one do they like the best?

Use the labels from an identical variety pack to make a 'my favourite cereal' pictogram.

After much discussion, the children will start to recognise the cereal packets both by name and picture. Draw attention to the name by discussing whether it is a good description of the cereal. Can the children match the variety-pack boxes to large cereal boxes of the same make?

After much free play with the boxes, cut out and mount just the names of the cereal and see if the children can match those from the variety pack with those from the large cereal boxes.

We've got one of those!

Objective

For children to be aware of printed words on electrical appliances.

What you need

Hair-drier, food processor, catalogues and brochures of electrical appliances, duplicating paper, photocopier, photocopiable page 90.

What to do

Take into school a couple of household electrical appliances, for example, a hair-drier and a food processor, and display them so that the children can examine them. Ask them to point out any writing they can see on the appliances and what they think it might say.

Have a brainstorming session with the children to think of as many household objects as possible that use electricity. What sort of instructions might be written on them?

Send home a copy of photocopiable page 90 and ask parents to help the children write down on the pictures the manufacturers of the appliances and a few of the instructions they find on them. When the sheets have been returned to school go on a tour of the school to examine all the instructions on the school electrical appliances.

NB It is important to warn the children about the dangers of playing with electricity sockets.

Books and more

Chapter three

Through careful monitoring of children's reading attitudes and behaviours (see Chapter five), teachers will know when planned teaching of specific reading strategies is necessary.

It is vital that parents help with their children's reading and this chapter begins with ideas for ensuring that parents are fully informed how best to do this. It continues with ideas for enabling children to understand the terminology of the reading process and provides ideas for maximising children's reading development through the use of teacher-made reading cards to supplement books and ensure individual motivation. There are also ideas for developing such strategies as using illustrations, semantic and syntactic cues to predict the text, and the acquisition of a vocabulary of sight words.

Helping parents to help

Objective

To enable parents to help their children become readers.

What you need

Duplicating facilities.

What to do

Arrange an evening for nursery and reception class parents designed to help them find out how they can help their children become readers. If possible, arrange for your local librarian or bookseller to be present to arrange a display of books.

You should structure the evening according to your requirements but you should try to cover the following key points:

● the importance of sharing rhymes, reading to children and chatting about books, from babyhood (perhaps nurseries could raise funds, or borrow books from the local library, to allow 'mother and toddler groups' to borrow books, as well as the nursery children);

● the value in talking about books without words;

● the nursery or infants' school's interpretation of shared/paired reading approaches (see 'Borrow a book', page 47);

● how children acquire a sight vocabulary, and how a school may send home games in addition to books to facilitate this;

● how parents can teach the alphabet (many children learn this simply by having an alphabet frieze in their bedroom), and the value of I-spy games (see also Chapter four).

● the place of word-building in the reading process — how the school teaches this, how parents can help with games (such as 30 second sessions with magnetic letters on the fridge), and how it is best not to interrupt children's enjoyment in reading aloud by getting them to sound out words (see also Chapter four).

Summarise these points in an attractive leaflet and give them out at the end of the evening.

Borrow a book

Objective

For parents to know how best to support children with the books they bring home.

What you need

Photocopier, paper, scissors, paper-clips.

What to do

Write and illustrate a set of flyers, which provide instructions for parents to follow when the children take a book home. For example:
● Please can you read this book to me, and have a chat about it?
● Let's read this book together, using shared reading.
● This is one of my old favourites. I think I can read it by myself.
● I think I can read this book on my own. Can you help me with the tricky bits?

You will be able to fit four flyers on to one sheet of A4 paper. The sheet can then be duplicated and cut up. When the children borrow a book the appropriate 'flyer' can then be attached to the front of the book with a paper-clip.

Book talk

Objective

To familiarise children with the terminology of the printed word, such as word, letter, sentence, space and so on.

What you need

Big books, metal board, card, felt-tipped pens, scissors, magnetic tape, magnetic letters, Blu-Tack.

What to do

Choose a popular page from a familiar big book, and point out to the children words, letters, spaces, sentences and so on. Copy out the page on to a piece of paper the same size as the metal board and stick the paper on to the metal board using Blu-Tack.

Increase the children's sight vocabulary by making small 'look and say' cards using some of the words from the page and stick magnetic tape on to the back of them. Give individual children a word each, to stick on the board, as you read from the big book.

If magnetic tape is unavailable, improvise by sticking the cards on to plastic magnetic letters with Blu-Tack. In addition, write each letter of the words of one sentence on separate card, and show the children how, by putting the letters together, the words are made. Alternatively, use magnetic letters to form the words.

Front-to-back

Objective

For children to understand that books work from front to back.

What you need

Big books, matching smaller books, individual books, children's video and video-recorder (optional), children's clothes.

What to do

Many children will come to appreciate the front-to-back nature of books simply from having many books read to them. However, children who have had little such experience may need a more explicit demonstration of this.

Stand a big book on an easel and discuss the front cover and the back cover with a group of children. Give them each a smaller format version of the same book and ask them to touch the front and back covers of their books.

After reading the story, talk about what happened at the beginning and end of the story. Explain to the children that the beginning is always found just after the front cover, and that the end of the story is always near the back cover. Let the children find the beginning and end of the stories in their books.

Have ready a selection of other books containing the words 'The end'. Mix these books in with books without these words, and let the children hunt for the special 'The end' books. Children are often fascinated by these words and they will eagerly search them out.

If possible, find a video and a matching story-book (for example, Postman Pat) and, for fun, play a short section of the film starting from the end, using 'rewind' (preferably starting with the words 'The end' if possible). Then, try reading the

book backwards, emphasising the absurdity of the task!

Follow-up

Explain that the front cover of a book is very useful for helping us to think about what the book is about. Demonstrate this by displaying a selection of books so that only their back covers are visible. Ask the children whether they can predict what any of the books are about!

Hold up the front covers of other books that are unfamiliar to the children and discuss what they think these books are about.

Left-to-right

Objective

For children to begin to appreciate the directionality of print.

What you need

A washing line or string, pegs, card, scissors, felt-tipped pens, crêpe paper, big books.

What to do

Write the first line of a nursery rhyme so that each word is on a separate large card. Peg them on a washing line and cover each card with a piece of crêpe paper.

Explain to the children that we read words in the same direction as we write. Ask the children to pretend to write the first line of this nursery rhyme. They can use their fingers in the air, from left to right, following your own right to left movements, as you face them. Ask the children to recite slowly the first line again. As they say each word, the children can point to it on the line, as you lift up the crêpe paper.

For fun, you and the children can say the words from right to left.

Follow-up

Give each child a word from a nursery rhyme written on a piece of card. Ask the children to sit in a row and as they say the rhyme, each child can stand up and hold up their word as it is said.

Word for word

Objective

For children to assimilate the one-to-one relationship between the spoken and written word.

What you need

Small Humpty Dumpty model (could be made from card), wooden or plastic building bricks, paper, sticky tape, felt-tipped pen, small sticky labels, old gloves.

What to do

Write out the first line of 'Humpty Dumpty' so that each word is on a separate piece of paper. Make sure that the paper is slightly smaller than the size of the bricks so that you can stick each word to a brick using sticky tape. The children can then say the rhyme and as they say each word they should pick up the relevant brick and place it on the floor, until the sentence is complete. Then Humpty Dumpty may be sat on top of the 'word wall'.

As reinforcement, the words may be written on small freezer labels, and each word stuck on the child's fingers, starting with the thumb of the left hand. As the child says each word, she should lift up the appropriate finger. As a next stage, the child can remove each word as you and the child recite the rhyme and stick them side-by-side on to a piece of paper.

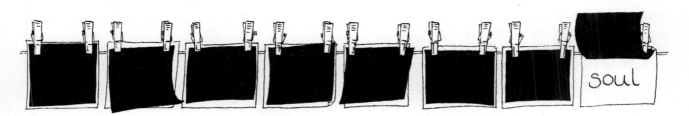

Reading pictures

Objective

To make children aware of picture clues when reading.

What you need

A variety of picture books without words, for example, *Sunshine* by Jan Ormerod (Puffin), comics, scissors, card, adhesive, clear self-adhesive plastic.

What to do

Give pairs of children a picture book to share between them. Let them talk about the pictures and the story to each other, before talking to you about it.

Cut up a story from a comic. Stick each frame on a separate piece of card and cover each card in clear self-adhesive plastic. Ask the pairs to try and put the pictures in order of the story sequence.

Bring in unusual pictures from newspapers, or interesting birthday or Christmas cards. Ask the children questions about the pictures so that you make up a group story about what could be happening, has already happened, or what might happen next.

Higgledy-piggledy

Objective

For children to appreciate the significance of word order.

What you need

Metal tray, magnetic tape or magnetic letters and Blu-Tack, card, scissors, felt-tipped pens.

What to do

Write out a three-word sentence, on separate cards, for example, 'Daniel loves mummy'. Stick magnetic tape to the back of each card and show the children how to assemble and reassemble sentences on the metal tray. For example, you could have 'Daniel loves mummy', 'Mummy loves Daniel' and, for fun, 'higgledy-piggledy' sentences such as: 'loves mummy Daniel'!

My story

Objectives

To reinforce sight vocabulary and encourage personal identification with books.

What you need

Children's books, paper, felt-tipped pen or printer.

What to do

This idea is particularly successful when used in conjunction with reading-scheme books. After a child has read a particular episode from a reading scheme, help him to imagine himself as a character in the story, and see if he can think of an alternative ending to the episode.

Write out a shortened and simplified version of the episode using the same vocabulary, but inserting the child's name and the alternative ending.

After reading this version, the child may enjoy dramatising it with friends.

My rhyme

Objective

To encourage focusing on separate words.

What you need

Paper, felt-tipped pens, scissors.

What to do

Help the child to choose a short favourite rhyme or limerick. Make sure that the child can read it using shared reading. Make two copies of the rhyme on paper, writing the words as large as possible. Cut up one of the copies into individual words and see whether the child can:
- place the individual words on top of the base words;
- lay out the words in order on a table, while referring to the other sheet for verification;
- eventually, put the words in order on the table, without reference to the other sheet.

Floor reading

Objective

To combine physical movement with the acquisition of a sight vocabulary and sentence-making skills.

What you need

Card, felt-tipped pens, scissors, Blu-Tack, sugar paper.

What to do

The space and opportunity for large physical movement is very important for young children and can provide strong motivation for simple reading games. On separate large cards write out simple sentences, such as the first line of a nursery rhyme or song that is well-known to the children. Write out, too, the individual words from each sentence, on smaller separate cards. Scatter all the small word cards from each sentence, one sentence at a time, over the carpet area. Read the sentence to the child and make sure the child can repeat it. Ask the child to say it again, this time pointing to each word on the large card, one at a time. Now ask the child to pick up the correct word card for each word one at a time. They should put them in the correct order on a large piece of sugar paper on the floor, referring to the large card if necessary.

Follow-up

A variation of this activity is to place the separate words on the playground or grass, or to stick them to a wall or all over a climbing frame with Blu-Tack, and ask a child to hunt out the words.

Rhyme bingo

Objective

The acquisition of a sight vocabulary and the fostering of group co-operative skills.

What you need

Sugar paper, felt-tipped pens, scissors, card.

What to do

Write out on sugar paper a nursery rhyme or song that the children know well. Cut the rhyme up into appropriate units, such as self-contained lines, phrases or sentences, and give each piece to a child. For example, if you used 'The Grand Old Duke of York', you would cut the paper into eight pieces, and give a piece to each child in a group of eight.

Sit the children round a table or in a circle on the carpet area. Hold up at random the words of the song which you have written out separately on small cards. Let the children help one another to identify each word, and see who has the matching word on his piece of paper. That child must then take the card and cover up the matching word on his piece of paper.

When all the words on the children's paper have been covered, ask them to give you back all the small word cards and then work together to put the pieces of paper in the correct order, one underneath the other, to make the complete rhyme or song.

Did you know?

Objective

For children to appreciate that reading can be a potent way of acquiring knowledge.

What you need

Children's encyclopaedias, comics, card, felt-tipped pens, clear self-adhesive plastic, scissors.

What to do

Find out about the children's interests (see page 10). Look in children's encyclopaedias and other reference books for a few fascinating facts on the various topics. For example, did the children know that some crocodiles will let small birds clean their teeth? Write out one fact on each card and illustrate it with a simple illustration and cover it with clear self-adhesive plastic. Entitle each card, 'Did you know that . . .', and let the children borrow the cards to take home and share with their parents. Write at the top of each card, 'Please read with me, using shared reading'.

How do you do it?

Objective

To encourage the children to pay close attention to the written word.

What you need

Card, felt-tipped pens, clear self-adhesive plastic or duplicated sheets.

What to do

On card, or duplicated sheets, write out simple, numbered instructions to enable the children to make, for example, a model on their own. Ensure that all the necessary materials are easily available in the classroom. Tell the children that they may ask one another for help with reading the instructions, but not you.

Additionally, simple recipes may be written on paper, for the children to carry out at home.

Guess the book

Objective

To develop children's oral skills in memorisation, precis and description.

What you need

Cardboard carton, wrapping paper, sticky tape, scissors, books.

What to do

Make a screen by flattening the carton, and covering it with colourful wrapping paper. Make sure that the screen will stand up on a table. Put a small selection of well-known story books on a table outside the room and let one of the children choose one she knows well. Let her look at it for a few moments, to refamiliarise herself with the contents, and then put the book in a carrier bag so that none of the other children can see it, and return with the child to the room.

Place the book flat on the table behind the screen, where only the child who chose it can see it. She should then try to describe the book (plot, characters, places, pictures and so on) without mentioning the name of the book, to the rest of the children who should try to guess the title.

The child may open the book, as an aid to memory, although some children may be able to talk about the book without opening it.

Play it again

Objective

To enable children to develop the habit of mentally responding to what they read.

What you need

Selection of children's videos and related story-books, sugar paper, felt-tipped pens, stapler.

What to do

Play a short snippet from a children's video and ask the children to guess what they think had happened previously and what might happen next. Read the corresponding section in the related book, and ask the same questions. Stress that there are no wrong answers, only alternatives, which can all make interesting stories.

Write some of these suggestions down in class story-books.

Rhyme lines

Objective
To encourage word recognition and ordering skills.

What you need
A collection of small toys or pictures, card, felt-tipped pens, scissors.

What to do
Think of the first lines of nursery rhymes which contain a mixture of nouns and other parts of speech, for example:
- Jack and Jill went up the hill;
- Polly put the kettle on;
- The wheels on the bus go round and round;
- Old Mother Hubbard went to the cupboard;
- Humpty Dumpty sat on a wall;
- Jelly on a plate, jelly on a plate — Wibble wobble, wibble wobble, Jelly on a plate (use the whole of this rhyme).

Collect appropriate small toys or pictures to represent the nouns.

For each first line, write out all the non-noun words on separate cards. In addition, write out each first line on a large piece of card. Ask the child to repeat one first line after you, and then to say it again, pointing one at a time, to each word on the large piece of card.

Show the child how you line up the relevant toys and word cards in the correct order on the table, and then ask the child to do the same. Let the child look at the large piece of card for reference. For example, with 'The wheels on the bus', the child should first put down the word 'The', followed by a small collection of toy wheels. Then the child should place the words 'on' and 'the', followed by a toy bus, and then the words 'go' and 'round'. Children soon come to understand that we can't have a toy to show some of the words, and so we have to write them down on cards, instead.

Hunt that word

Objective
To reinforce whole word recognition.

What you need
Card, plastic wallets, highlighter pens, scissors, Blu-Tack.

What to do
To reinforce important but 'colourless' words such as 'the', write out rhymes, such as 'Hey diddle diddle', on card, and put them into a clear plastic wallet. The child can then circle specific words on the plastic wallet, using a highlighter pen.

A page of a book can also be slipped directly into a wallet, or the wallet can be slit open and fixed on top of the page with paper-clips.

An alternative is to choose a page from a book that contains several examples of the 'colourless' word and, protecting the page using a plastic wallet, let the child cover up each example of the particular word using a matching word card.

This idea works well with a page from a big book, too. Cover it with a clear plastic sheet, and let the children either highlight the words, or stick the matching words on top using Blu-Tack.

Sticky words

Objective
To encourage word matching skills.

What you need
A roll of small white self-adhesive labels, scissors, sticky tape, felt-tipped pens, paper, children's books.

What to do
In order to reinforce the recognition of certain words in a child's reading programme, send home from time to time a 'sticky word-game' related to a child's book.

Choose a particular sentence from the child's book which contains words on which you wish to focus her attention. Write out the sentence on a piece of paper, underneath a simple drawing. Ensure that each word is no bigger than a sticky label. Next, copy out each word on to sticky labels, in random order. Cut off the strip of labels containing the words and attach it to the paper with sticky tape. Write a short instruction to parents to say that when the child has read the book, she should peel off the word labels and stick them on top of the matching words you have written and bring the sticky word-game to you to see.

What comes next?

Objective
To develop word-prediction skills.

What you need
Big books, card, felt-tipped pens, scissors, Blu-Tack, clear plastic wallet.

What to do
Read a page from a big book together with individual children or a group. Cover up the final word of a sentence, so that only the initial letter of the word is visible. See if the children can predict what this word is.

Prepare two or three cards with words beginning with the same initial letter as the missing word, but which would not make sense if substituted. Cover the page with clear plastic, and let the children have fun, sticking on the various words with Blu-Tack, and reading aloud the different sentences.

The missing word

Objective
To give children practice in semantic and syntactic cueing.

What you need
Card, felt-tipped pens, scissors, plastic wallets, Blu-Tack, clear self-adhesive film, small freezer labels.

What to do
Give children some simple cloze-procedure games. Write out on A4 card very short stories, based on characters in reading schemes or familiar story books. Leave blank spaces instead of certain words and slip the cards into plastic wallets. Write out the missing words on small cards and cover them with clear self-adhesive plastic. Let the children work in pairs to stick the missing words in the correct places, using small balls of Blu-Tack.

For added interest, make one or two of these games, floor-sized, for the children to work with on the carpet. Similarly, cover a page from a big book with a sheet of clear self-adhesive plastic and blank out several words using white sticky labels. Write out these words on small cards and let the children stick them in the correct places with Blu-tack.

What are they saying?

Objectives
To encourage children to empathise with book characters and to reinforce sight vocabulary.

What you need
Paper, felt-tipped pens, scissors, Blu-Tack, books including big books, large pictures, clear self-adhesive plastic, clear plastic wallets.

What to do
Choose pictures from books that show different characters talking. Ask the children for their ideas about what the characters in the pictures might be saying. Write the children's suggestions in speech bubbles and cut them out. Protecting the pictures from the books with transparent plastic sheets and clear wallets, let the children stick the speech bubbles next to the appropriate characters, using Blu-Tack, and read out the words.

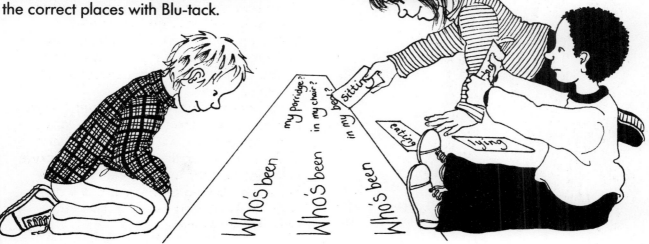

A to Z

Chapter four

Research has shown that there is a correlation between the number of alphabet letters children know on entry to school and their later reading ability (Blachford *et al*, 1987). The teaching of the alphabet has always been highly valued by parents, and nursery and infant teachers are in a strong position to capitalise on this.

The same research has also revealed that children who have been taught the names of capital letters at home do not become confused at school but, rather, are at an advantage by the end of the reception year (Blatchford *et al*, 1987).

The ideas in this chapter include activities that involve parents, children's physical movement, listening games as a prerequisite to word building, and activities to facilitate children's independent use of phonic skills in their reading.

If your name begins with 'A'

Objective
To encourage children to recognise the first sound of their name.

What you need
Card, crayons, felt-tipped pen, sticky tape, collage materials.

What to do
Help the children begin to learn the first sound of their names by letting them make name badges. Write each child's name in the centre of a piece of card, saying the name out loud as you write and emphasising the initial sound. The children can then decorate round the edge of the name with collage materials or crayons.

Before the children stick the sticky tape on the back of the badge, play some recognition games. Place the badges on group tables and give each child a matching name card to hold. Tell them to go and sit in the place marked by their badge. This system is an effective way of grouping children as they return to the class from outdoor play.

When the children are wearing their badges play set games to develop listening skills. For example, when the children are all gathered together just before lunch, send them off in small groups by saying 'All the children whose name begins with "A" go and wash your hands'. Alternatively, ask the children to perform certain actions, for example, stand up and clap your hands three times if your name begins with 'D'.

Follow-up
See if the children can group themselves according to the initial sound of their first names.

Alphabet corners

Objective

To relate initial sounds to words and objects in a fun music game.

What you need

Large pieces of paper, Blu-Tack, felt-tipped pen, card, cassette player, music tape, use of a large space such as a hall or gymnasium.

What to do

Draw four letters on four large pieces of paper avoiding putting similar ones, such as b, d, p, q, in the same game. Stick the letters up on the walls on different sides of the room at child height. Tell the children to dance, hop and skip while the music is playing and when the music stops they could:
- look at the alphabet card you hold up and run to the identical letter;
- look at the picture or object you hold up and run to the initial sound;
- listen to the word you say and run to its initial sound.

With all these games the last three children to reach the letter are out until the few remaining children become joint winners.

Follow-up

To develop the game you could stick up letter blends such as: sh, st, pr, ch.

Beat the timer

Objective

To encourage children to associate initial sounds with objects in their classroom environment.

What you need

Large plastic letters (lower case), Blu-Tack, minute timer.

What to do

Strategically place a number of objects around the classroom at child height. Tell the children that you are going to give them five plastic letter 'a's', 'b's' and so on, with Blu-Tack attached to the back of them. Can they take turns to label five objects in the classroom beginning with that sound before the timer runs out?

Tidy up letter game

Objective

To develop an awareness of the initial sound of classroom games.

What you need

Small self-adhesive labels, or rings with mounted sticky labels attached.

What to do

At the end of a work session encourage the children to think about the initial sounds of the equipment they have been using or the games they have been playing. Give each child a letter label to stick on the back of their hands or a ring with a mounted letter label attached to it to wear on their fingers. They must then try to work out which game or piece of equipment begins with that initial sound and go and tidy it away.

Alphabet picnic

Objective

To teach initial sounds and letters.

What you need

A rug, food items or pictures of food, a roll of sticky labels, felt-tipped pens, paper napkins (optional), picnic hamper (optional), paper, scissors.

What to do

Spread the rug on the carpet area, and give each child a paper napkin on which has been written a different alphabet letter. If no napkins are available, give each child a sticky label with a letter written on it to stick on their hands.

Fill the hamper with various food items or pictures of food, making sure that there are three items beginning with each child's letter. Ask each child in turn to come to the hamper and select all the food items beginning with his letter. The children can then place their items on their paper napkin.

For reinforcement, the children can stick a letter label on to each food item. Ask them to say the name of the food and its initial sound as they do so.

Alphabet trail

Objective

To associate objects with their initial sounds with the help of an alphabet trail.

What you need

Gloss paint or chalk, paint brush, dice.

What to do

Paint or chalk an alphabet trail on the nursery or school playground and use it for a variety of games. For example:
• Throw a die to determine how many spaces the children must jump. When they land on a letter they must say a word beginning with that sound or else miss a turn. The child to reach the end of the trail first is the winner.
• Take a box of objects outside and ask the children to match up all the objects with their initial letters. Alternatively, give the children an identical box of objects each and let them throw a die to determine how many objects they should match with a letter each go. The winner is the first child to empty her box.

Personalised alphabet books

Objective

To learn the alphabet sounds through words that have personal meaning to each child.

What you need

Duplicating paper, photocopier, a copy of *Lucy and Tom's ABC* by Shirley Hughes.

What to do

Read *Lucy and Tom's ABC* to the children and encourage them to talk about objects and experiences which are important to them.

Send a letter to parents asking them to jot down words related to each letter of the alphabet that have personal significance for their child.

Use this information to write out an alphabet booklet for each child letting the children illustrate each word.

Use these booklets at news time or story time to help children talk about their interests.

Alphabet name books

Objective

To teach capital letters in alphabetical order.

What you need

Large coloured sugar-paper book, white paper, felt-tipped pen, adhesive.

What to do

Make a class alphabet book of the children's first names by printing their names on individual pieces of paper and letting the children draw a picture of themselves. (Alternatively send home a request for a recent photograph of each child.) Mount the names and pictures in alphabetical order in the sugar-paper book, ensuring that the relevant capital letter is printed at the top of each page. If no name starts with a particular letter leave the page blank apart from the letter at the top.

Make a similar class book using the children's surnames.

Follow-up

Rearrange the children's names in the cloakroom area into alphabetical order of either first name or surname. The children will soon learn whether their name comes at the beginning, middle or end of the alphabet.

Tongue-twister alphabet book

Objective
To teach initial sounds and letters.

What you need
White paper, felt-tipped pens, scissors, a hole punch, ribbon, sugar paper.

What to do
Make up a simple tongue-twister for each child, preferably with three words starting with the same letter, although two will suffice if three are not possible. Use the children's names where possible, but try to cover all the letters of the alphabet. Some examples are:
• Suleman sits on a see-saw;
• Jason jumps in a jelly;
• Pooja plays in a pool;
• Tracy jumps on a trampoline;
• Michael eats a melon;
• Daniel plays a drum.

Write the sentences on paper and let each child illustrate her own tongue-twister. Stick them all in a 'Tongue-twister alphabet book', covering the book in sugar paper and securing the pages with a ribbon.

I-spy riddles

Objective
To match initial sounds to objects through playing a simplified I-spy game.

What you need
Objects beginning with four or five different sounds, tray.

What to do
Place about five familiar objects on a tray, making sure that they all begin with a different sound. Working with a small group of children, start off the game by giving both the sound and a short description of one of the objects. For example: 'I-spy something beginning with "b" that is a fruit and we have to peel'.

As the children become more proficient at the game, limit the clues that are given until only the initial sound is given. Change the objects regularly until the whole alphabet is covered.

Mystery hunt

Objective

To encourage children to think of a variety of objects beginning with each sound.

What you need

Card, a selection of treasures, sticky tape, string.

What to do

Put a teddy on a low branch of a tree or somewhere fairly noticeable, but not too obvious en route from the school entrance to the classroom. Place a sign on the school gate asking parents and children to look carefully to see if they can find something beginning with 't' in an unusual place before they reach the classroom door.

Encourage parents to play the same game at home. For example, can their child see something beginning with 's' before he washes his face?

Follow-up

Use this game to introduce a 'sound for the day' with a variety of activities being based around that letter.

Hunt the letter

Objective

To help children discriminate between letters in a fun race situation.

What you need

A tin of alphabet spaghetti, spoons, plastic bowls.

What to do

Line up a group of children in a large space at the far end of the school hall and give each child a little plastic bowl of alphabet spaghetti and a spoon. Tell

them that they are going to have a race to find different letters of the alphabet. Name a letter sound and the children must carefully dip into their spaghetti with their spoons to find the letter. When they have found the letter they should race towards you with it.

The game can be concluded by everyone eating their remaining letters, naming the letter sound to their partners before the spoon goes into their mouths!

Odd one out

Objective

To increase awareness of the difference between initial sounds.

What you need

Name badges.

What to do

Stand four children at the front of the classroom. Make sure that three of their names begin with the same initial letter, the other being the 'odd one out'. Ask the children which child they think is different from the other three. Let them work out lots of differences before giving them a few clues about sounds. Can they find the 'odd one out'?

This game could, of course, be simplified by the children wearing name badges.

Follow-up

See whether the children can find the 'odd one out' from groups of three or four objects.

Letter-boxes

Objectives
To encourage children to relate objects to their printed initial sound.

What you need
Twenty-six small cuboid wooden or cardboard boxes, paper, felt-tipped pen, small objects beginning with each sound of the alphabet.

What to do
Remove the lids from the boxes and label the sides with each lower case letter of the alphabet. Show the children the objects and ask them to name each object, to ensure that there is no misunderstanding. Using about four boxes and four objects at a time let a small group of children put each object in the correct box, for example, the little ball in the 'b' box and so on. Change the boxes and objects frequently until they have all been matched.

Letter-die lotto

Objective
To relate sound to object within the context of a lotto game.

What you need
A large foam die, sticky tape, thick paper, felt-tipped pen, ruler, card.

What to do
Adapt a large foam die by attaching a lower-case letter label to each of its sides with sticky tape, and draw a line under the base of each letter to avoid confusion. Make four simple lotto type cards containing pictures of objects starting with the six different sounds on the die.

Four children can then take turns to throw the die, name the sound and put a counter on the relevant picture on their card. If they already have a counter on that letter they should miss a turn.

Change the letters on the die and make more lotto cards until all the initial sounds of the alphabet have been learned.

An alternative to this is to put a number of objects on a tray and let the children take an object according to the throw on the letter die. When the tray is empty the child with the most objects is the winner.

Tap your name

Objective

To help children begin to break down words into separate syllables.

What you need

A tambourine or drum.

What to do

Sit the children in a circle and ask them to listen very carefully as you tap out the rhythm of your name on the tambourine. Demonstrate one or two of the children's names and then pass the tambourine round the circle letting each child take a turn to tap out their name. To begin with, concentrate on first names, but as the children become more experienced include their surnames as well. As the children become even more proficient at tapping out separate syllables see if they can echo you as you tap out the first line of a well-known nursery rhyme.

Can they recognise whole rhymes or songs tapped out on the tambourine? After a few weeks practice, they too will become proficient at tapping out their chosen rhymes. This new ability can form the basis of 'name that tune' class quizes.

Rhyme time

Objective

For children to appreciate the concept of rhyming words.

What you need

Toys, household objects, percussion instruments, paper, felt-tipped pens, magnetic letters, metal board, sticky tape.

What to do

It has been shown that children who have difficulty recognising a rhyme, can experience reading difficulties later on, especially with phonic skills (Bradley and Bryant, 1983). Some ideas to help children assimilate this concept are:
● Recite rhymes, pausing before the rhyming words for the child to complete.
● Give the child a percussion instrument to bang when she hears the rhyming words as you recite them.

- Put objects which rhyme in pairs (or use drawings). Let the children say the names of the objects, and put them side by side to form rhyming pairs. Deliberately put two objects together which do not rhyme, and ask if they rhyme.
- Take two of the rhyming objects or pictures and tell the children that you are going to make up a funny rhyme about the two things. For example: 'I played with my top. Then I got out my mop'. Pause to let the child say the final rhyming words.
- Take two rhyming objects and draw them one beneath the other. Stick the drawing on to a metal board with sticky tape. Using magnetic letters, make the words, one under the other, and point out how only the first letters are different. You can then leave one word and carry on changing the first letter of the other to make other rhyming words.

Sound segment cards

Objective
To enable children to hear separate sounds within words.

What you need
Card, felt-tipped pens, ruler, counters, plastic or magnetic letters.

What to do
Make a few picture cards to illustrate simple words (or hold up the real objects). For each word or object make another card divided into squares, one for each sound in the word (not letter), for example, me, boy (two squares), cat, boat, ship, house (three squares), train, jump (four squares).

Hold up one picture or object and say the word slowly and deliberately. Help the child to do the same, putting a counter in each square for each sound articulated.

Do the activity together for as long as necessary, and accept the child's approximations until eventually they become more co-ordinated.

Older children can use plastic or magnetic letters instead of counters in the squares.

(This idea is taken from *The Early Detection of Reading Difficulties* by Marie Clay.)

Verbal pingpong

Objective
To encourage children to put sounds together to make two-letter words.

What you need
Card, thick felt-tipped pen, a large working area, an adult helper.

What to do
Break up well-known two-letter words, for example, 'in', 'at', 'on' and 'is', to make two-piece jigsaws. Take the children into a large space and ask them to sit down. Give a piece of card with one letter of a two-letter jigsaw to an adult helper and holding the other piece yourself stand a few metres apart.

Play verbal pingpong by saying the first sound of the word and your helper saying the second sound. The first child to work out the word can put the jigsaw together. Ask the children to repeat the word as they look at the completed jigsaw.

This game can be played with three letter words using three piece jigsaws and two helpers.

Magnetic words

Objective
To encourage two-letter word building through the use of magnetic letters.

What you need
Paper, magnet boards, lower case magnetic letters, paper-clip or Blu-Tack, felt-tipped pens.

What to do
Print out and illustrate the first lines of a well-known nursery rhyme on to individual pieces of paper, replacing two-letter words with two dashes, for example, 'Humpty Dumpty sat — — a wall'. Attach the paper to small magnet boards using a paper-clip or Blu-Tack. Read the lines with the children pausing to let them say the missing two-letter words. Ask them to find the missing letters from a tray of about six magnetic letters and see if they can place them in the correct order on the magnet board.

Baby talk

Objective
To focus children's attention on two-letter sound blending.

What you need
Paper, felt-tipped pens, card, scissors, a photocopier, magnetic letters, a metal tray.

What to do
Talk with the children about the sounds babies make before they can speak properly. Mention specifically 'ba ba, da da, ha ha, ma ma'. Ask a child to articulate these sounds, while composing them with magnetic letters on a metal tray.

Draw a picture of a happy baby with a blank speech bubble coming from the baby's mouth. Photocopy this picture, and have ready some speech-bubble shaped cards containing the baby sounds you have discussed. Ask a child to place one speech bubble on each duplicated baby picture, telling you what the sounds are. If the child is able, he may also copy the sounds inside the bubbles.

Reading bricks

Objective
For children to focus closely on phonic word-building.

What you need
Small cards, or paper and scissors, sticky labels, sticky tape, felt-tipped pens.

What to do
Select a group of words, all beginning with the same two or three letters. Draw simple, amusing pictures on separate cards, or pieces of paper, to indicate different meanings. For example, draw a picture of a cat sitting on a mat or a rat sitting on top of a hat and so on. Write all the words (including 'the' and 'a') on large sticky labels (or use paper and sticky tape) and stick each word separately to the side of a wooden or plastic brick (the larger the better). Give the child one picture and ask him to say what is happening in each picture, for example, 'The duck dug into the mud' and then put the bricks in the correct order on the floor.

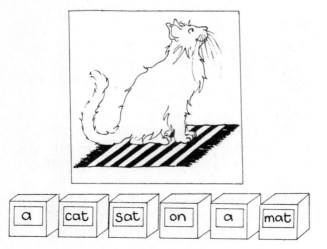

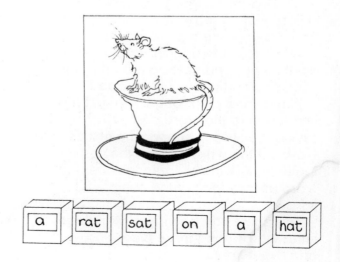

Prime words

Objective

To facilitate a child's two- and three-letter word building, prior to her own reading.

What you need

Small cards, or paper and scissors, felt-tipped pens, children's books.

What to do

Before you, or a parent, read a book, or section, to the children you should read it to yourself first. Jot down any suitable phonic words on which you wish to focus the child's attention. (For this idea, books from phonic reading schemes are especially appropriate.) Write these words on separate cards or pieces of paper and just before reading the book with the child say, 'I've just read this book myself and it's all about . . .'. As you give the synopsis of the story, pause dramatically before a phonic word, and put it on the table in front of the child, and see if she can read it herself. Heighten the anticipation (and reading value!) by covering up all but the first letter, or two, or three, and slowly reveal them.

As the child's phonic skills develop, you can offer a choice of two or even three words on the table.

Peeping letters

Objective

To enable children to use initial phonic building in their own reading.

What you need

Sets of four identical story-books, card, scissors, paper, felt-tipped pens.

What to do

Choose a story with which the children are familiar. Jot down from the story a selection of words whose initial letters are appropriate for phonic building. Write each word on a large piece of card, and also four times on small cards or pieces of paper the same size as the print in the books.

Before you read each page aloud with the group, hold up one of the words on a large card, with all but the initial letters covered with a piece of blank card. See if the children can work out the word just from this 'peeping' initial letter.

Next, give each child the small version of the word, blank side up. Ask them to point to the word on their page, and to cover up all but the initial 'peeping' letter, as you did. They should read this letter, then the whole word, and finally turn over the small card and place it on the word.

Growing readers

Chapter five

'The record of the continuous assessment should cover what the child has read; the child's reading strategies and approaches when handling a familiar text, levels of comprehension; retrieval of information; and the child's reading tastes and preferences' (*English for ages 5 to 16*, HMSO, para 16.48). The ongoing monitoring of a child's growth as a reader in this way must actively involve the child, parents and teacher together. Although schools will have their own systems for keeping records of assessment, it is suggested in this chapter that, as a complement to them, an informal 'reading diary' is kept for each child at the infant stage.

This gives tangible form to the working relationship between child, parent(s) and teacher, and ensures that decisions made by the teacher concerning the planned next steps of reading tuition for the child, are clearly communicated to the parent(s), who will then be in a strong position to reinforce the teacher's work in the home. Additionally, the reading diary gives the child opportunities to contribute, thereby strengthening her self-image as a reader.

The chapter begins with a description of a reading record for nursery children, which involves them and their parents, and which can constitute the first entries in the reading diary on transfer to infant school. After describing various ways in which the reading diary can be used at infant school, the chapter concludes with descriptions of three early years' reading tests, for beginning, emergent and newly-independent readers.

and allocate two copies for each child. When a child starts nursery, explain the record to her parents, and give them a copy to keep, so that they may have an 'overview' of their child's reading development. Keep the other copy at nursery and from time to time, arrange to see the child's parent(s), so that together you may discuss the child's growth as a reader. Colour in the appropriate petals with a highlighter pen.

As you fill in the record with the parents, try to involve the child in the conversation as much as possible, so that she appreciates that she is the focus of attention as a reader. Give the child a blank version of the record sheet and as you fill in the petals on the flower show the child her flower and ask her to tell you about it. She could also bring you a favourite book and write in the title on one of the petals, and then colour in that petal herself.

Do this on each occasion, so that by the time the child leaves nursery, her flower record will be completed, with the names of lots of favourite books.

Shared records

Objective
To involve children and parents of nursery-aged children in encouraging their children to read.

What you need
Photocopiable page 91, highlighter pens.

What to do
Photocopy the reading record on page 91 (devised by Caroline Matusiak, 'Shared Records', *Child Education* November 1988), or design your own

Reading diary

Objective

To have a tangible record of the three-way relationship between child, parent and teacher, in developing a child's reading at the infant stage.

What you need

Plain exercise books, publishers' catalogues, felt-tipped pens, clear self-adhesive plastic.

What to do

The reading diary is a working document that is shared between the child, parent(s) and teacher. It covers all aspects of how parents and teachers work together to help the child become a reader. An important aspect of the diary is that it should be 'user-friendly', that is, informal, jargon-free and often anecdotal, with contributions from the child. Use the diary not only as a record of books that have been read, with comments from parents and child, but also as a way of ensuring that parental help is 'targeted' as accurately as possible. Curriculum demands can mean that the time available for planned reading tuition at school is at a premium. This means that reinforcement activities that are planned and monitored by you, but carried out at home by the parent(s), and communicated via the diary, can be extremely valuable. The advantages to the children, of maximising parental help by means of the diary far outweigh any seemingly extra work-load involved in writing it. From time to time, a short chat, either before or after school, with a parent, to amplify a point, is well worth it. Examples of the kind of comment a teacher could write in the reading diary are:

- 'Aisha has been enjoying playing I-spy. Please could you continue at home.'
- 'Now that Mark knows all his alphabet letters, I have been encouraging him to look at the first letters of new words, as a clue. Please could you continue this, and jot down how he gets on over the next few weeks.'
- 'As I mentioned to you yesterday, so that Emma doesn't come to see reading as a chore by having to sound out new words in her reading, please could you give her a head start by playing the "prime words" game I described (words in Emma's book wallet), before she reads tonight's book.'

• 'I have been asking Julia a lot of 'why?' questions about her books, recently, to encourage her to think about the meaning. She chose *I Don't Feel Well* today. Please could you read it to her. Ask her why she thinks Elizabeth is looking so cross when her brother is ill, and jot down what she says.'

• 'We have been playing "hunt the letter". Please could you say a letter, and see if David can find it in this alphabet book. Then let him ask you to 'hunt the letter' and so on.'

• 'As Suliman brought his sun-glasses to school today, I thought he might enjoy *Bethy Wants a Blue Ice-cream*. We have looked through coloured plastic discs. If you have any coloured sweet paper, perhaps you could do this too?'

Whenever you use a test on a child make sure that you write a summary of your observations of the child's reading strategies and your proposals for future action, in the diary. Ideally, the diary should begin with copies of the nursery reading record (both the adults' and children's) stuck on the first two pages.

Make the cover colourful and attractive. If possible, let the child decorate it by sticking on small pictures of books cut from publishers' catalogues or by drawing a picture. Cover the diary with self-adhesive plastic.

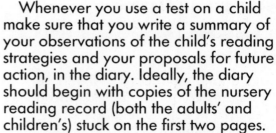

Child's say

Objective

To enable a child to contribute to his reading diary.

What you need

Smiley stickers, or plain circular stickers, felt-tipped pens, photocopier.

What to do

So that the child values his diary and feels a sense of ownership in it, think of ways for him to make contributions, based on his growing awareness of himself as a reader. Some suggestions for ways to do this follow.

• Use stickers, either commercially produced or hand drawn on plain round stickers, showing smiley faces and sad faces. From time to time, let the child put a sticker next to a book title, to show whether he enjoyed it or not. The parent can jot down what she had to say about the book too.

• Make a simple outline drawing (about 10 × 10cm) of a child and parent sharing a book, with two empty speech bubbles. Draw several of these drawings on an A4 sheet, and photocopy as often as required. Cut out the pictures and occasionally stick one in the child's diary. Write the title of a recently read book on the 'book front' in the drawing, and, having asked the child first what he thought about the book, write his comment in his speech bubble. In the adult's speech bubble, write what your question was.

• Occasionally, let the child draw a picture in the diary about a favourite character or showing an alternative ending.

Lists and lists

Objective
To encourage children to think about their preferences in books.

What you need
Paper, a pen, scissors, adhesive.

What to do
Some children very much enjoy reading or listening to series of books, or books about the same subject. The books may come from school, home or a public library.

On paper, copy out the titles of sets of books on subjects in which the child is showing an interest. Cut out the titles and stick them in the child's reading diary. Next to each title, draw a square or book shape for the child to colour each time that title is read or heard.

Give each list of titles a heading, for example:

• Dr Seuss books I can read;
• Books about bears I can read;
• 1, 2, 3 and Away! books I can read;
• Alfie books I enjoy hearing;
• Postman Pat books I enjoy hearing.

Favourite five

Objective

To acknowledge a child's personal choice in books.

What you need

Photocopiable page 92, paper, a pen, a ruler, children's books, book catalogues.

What to do

This is a book-based child's version of the 'Desert Island Discs' idea. At the end of the reception year, ask the children to imagine that they are going on an exciting holiday to the moon with their family. Tell them that the journey will be a long one, and that they will need to take along five of their favourite books. Let the children look at library books and book catalogues, as well as their reading diaries, to jog their memories.

Make copies of the moon rocket on photocopiable page 92, and ask the children to fill in the title of each book in the blank spaces of the rocket.

Hear all about it

Objective

To reinforce a child's self-image as a reader, and to provide information which will contribute towards a teacher's formative assessment at the end of the reception year.

What you need

A photocopier, paper, a typewriter or pen, blank audio cassettes from parents, a tape recorder, a child's favourite book, paper.

What to do

At the end of the reception year, help each child to make a short 'book review' on tape in which she briefly talks about her favourite book and chooses a short passage from it to read aloud.

In June or July, send a letter home to parents, asking them, if possible, to send in a blank audio cassette tape. Discuss with each child which book she would enjoy reading aloud from, with reference to her reading diary. Encourage the child to choose a book she knows she can read very well indeed even if, or especially if, she knows it 'off by heart'! Tell the child she is going to make a 'radio programme' about the book. Talk with her about the title of the book, its author, what happens, her favourite part or character and so on, and jot down what she says. From your notes, write out for her a very simple 'review', along these lines:

- My favourite book is called . . . .
- It is by . . . .
- In the book (say what happens or what it's about) . . . .
- My favourite part of the book/ person/animal is . . . .
- Now I am going to read some of the book for you . . . .

Practise the reading of the 'review', and her favourite passage, with the child, using shared or paired reading, until she feels happy to record it.

The small amount of preliminary work necessary between child and teacher is enjoyable, and also provides the teacher with valuable information about the child as a reader. The information is presented in a form which will be treasured by children and parents.

Play two or three of these 'radio programmes' at a time to the whole class, or to the whole school at assembly time. They will very much enjoy listening to them.

Concepts about print: test

Objective

To assess a child's understanding of significant concepts about the printed language during the reception year.

What you need

A copy of Professor Marie Clay's book *Sand and Stones* or two very easy books, photocopiable page 93.

What to do

Use the following questions (from *The Early Detection of Reading Difficulties* by Marie Clay), or devise your own, to ascertain whether the children understand the following concepts: front of book, letter, word, formation of the space, that the print tells the story, big and little letters, first letter in word, use of punctuation, left to right orientation and line sequence.

1. Show me the front of this book.
2. I'll read this story. You help me. Show me where to start reading. Where do I begin to read?
3. Show me where to start.
4. Which way do I go?
5. Where do I go after that?
6. Point to it while I read it. (Word by word pointing.)
7. Show me the first part of the story. Show me the last part.
8. Show me the bottom of the picture.
9. Where do I begin?
Which way do I go?
Where do I go after that?
10. What's wrong with this? (Line sequence. Read immediately the bottom line first and then the top line. Do not point.)
11. Where do I start reading? (Read a left-hand page before a right-hand one.)

12. What's wrong on this page? (Word sequence.)
13. What's wrong on this page? (Point to the page number, *not* the text.)
14. What's wrong with the writing on this page? (Reordering letters within a word.)
15. What's this for? (Point to or trace the question mark with a finger or pencil.)
16. What's this for? (Point to or trace with a pencil the full stop.)
17. What's this for? (Point to or trace with a pencil the comma.)
18. What's this for? (Point to or trace with a pencil the quotation marks.)
19. Find a little letter like this.
20. Show me 'was'. Show me 'no'. (Reversible words.)

21. Push the cards (have two cards 13 × 15cm) across the story until all you can see is just one letter. Now show me two letters.

22. Show me just one word. Now show me two words. (Word concepts.)

23. Show me the first letter of a word. Show me the last letter of a word. (First and last letter concepts.)

24. Show me a capital letter.

Relate these questions to the score sheet on photocopiable page 93.

If desired, make two copies of your record of this test. One may be stuck in the child's reading diary, to be discussed with parents, and one kept by you.

book will usually provide the instructional level. Use the running record sheet on photocopiable page 94 to make running records, on transcripts of the passages, of the child's reading strategies at these three different levels. Use ticks for each correct response and record every error in full. Ask yourself what strategies the child was using, especially to tackle words she did not immediately recognise. Did she use picture clues or did she try to sound out the word? Diagnostic information comes from looking at the errors, including those that were self-corrected. Define the errors in terms of meaning (does the word make sense in

Running records

Objective

To give a formative reading assessment for emergent readers.

What you need

Children's books, paper, pen, photocopiable page 94.

What to do

A running record will establish a record of a child's level of independent reading, and also a formative assessment, giving information for future action. Choose a passage between 100 and 200 words long, from a child's book. If possible, choose passages from books of at least three levels of difficulty – easy (of which the child should be able to read 95% to 100% correctly), instructional (90% to 94% read correctly, and hard (80% to 89% read correctly). The child's current

the context?) structure (is it the right sort of word linguistically?), visual (is there evidence of attention to visual clues including letter/sound link?). An analysis of the errors made in the child's reading of the three samples will provide important information about the child's strengths (on the easier texts) and weaknesses (on the more difficult materials), and will help you to decide on future action. Write a summary of your conclusions in the child's diary.

The Early Detection of Reading Difficulties by Marie Clay gives comprehensive advice for a reading recovery programme for children whose reading performance, at the age of six years, may be giving cause for concern.

columns according to whether the substituted word is similar or dissimilar according to:
- sound — usually the same initial sound;
- look — the length and shape of the word;
- part of speech — verb for verbs, noun for noun and so on;
- meaning — is the meaning of the original word retained?

Tally the number of times the child refuses to try to read a word. This will reveal whether or not the child is confident enough to try and read new words, even though he may make mistakes.

There is an optional numerical calculation to show whether the text is too difficult for the child or not. Add the number of refusals to the number of substitutions made which lose the meaning, and see how this translates into a reading competence level as shown in the illustration below.

Miscue made simple

Objective
To give a formative reading assessment for children who have started to read independently.

What you need
Photocopiable page 95.

What to do
Listen to a child reading a passage of between 120 to 450 words. Each time the child substitutes one word for another, jot it down on the recording form on photocopiable page 95 (devised by Cliff Moon *Assessing Reading Strategies at Key Stage 1*, University of Reading, 1991). When the child has finished reading, tick and cross in the four

Name __Matthew__   Age __7__
Title and page(s) of book __Goldilocks and the Three Bears__   Class __5__
Year __2__
Date __16 March__

Substitutions

	Word printed	Word read	Sound	Look	Part of speech	Meaning
1	Little	Small				
2	Tiny	small	✗	✗	✓	✓
3	well	but	✗	✗	✓	✓
4	never	not	✓	✗	✓	✓
5						
6						
7						
8						
9						
10						
11						
12						

Tally of refusals		ЖНТ I

Negative miscue rate = $\frac{\text{Meaning errors} + \text{refusals}}{\text{Total number of words read}} \times 100 = \frac{6}{178} \times 100$

= 3.4 %

Level = Independent/instructional/frustration
      (1%) ↑   (5%)   (10%)

Notes on miscue analysis Readability of book about right; encourage him to attempt words. Same consonant work?

[From *Assessing Reading Strategies at Key Stage 1* by Cliff Moon, Reading and Language Centre, University of Reading, 1991.]

Book list

Children's books

Ahlberg, J. and Ahlberg, A. (1985) *Baby's Catalogue*, Viking Kestrel.

Brandenberg, F. (1982) *I Don't Feel Well*, Picture Puffin.

Gillham, B. (1986) *Bethy Wants a Blue Ice-cream*, Methuen.

Gretz, S. (1988) *Bears Who Went to the Seaside*, Black.

Hughes, S. (1986) *Lucy and Tom's ABC*, Picture Puffin.

Matterson, E. (ed.) (1969) *This Little Puffin*, Puffin Books.

Murphy, J. (1985) *Whatever Next!*, Macmillan.

Nicoll, H. and Pienkowski, J. (1976) *Meg at Sea*, Picture Puffin.

Ormerod, J. (1983) *Sunshine*, Picture Puffin.

Watanabe, S. (1981) *How Do I Put it on?*, Picture Puffin.

Reference books

Blatchford, P., Burke, J., Farquhar, C., Plewis, I. and Tizard, B. (1987) 'Associations between pre-school reading related skills and later reading achievement', *British Educational Research Journal*, 13(1), 15-23.

Bradley, L. and Bryant, P. (1983) *Reading Skills in Young Children and the Recognition of Auditory Similarities*. Final report to the Social Science Research Council, SSRC.

Clay, M. (1981) *The Early Detection of Reading Difficulties*, Heinemann Educational.

Clay, M. (1982) *Sand and Stones: Two Conceptual Print Tests*, Heinemann Educational.

Department of Education and Science (1989) *English for Ages 5 to 16* HMSO.

Hohmann, M., Banet, B. and Weikart, D. P. (1979) *Young Children in Action*, The High/Scope Press.

Matusiak, C. (1988) 'Shared records', *Child Education*, November.

Moon, C. (1991) *Assessing Reading Strategies at Key Stage 1*, Reading and Language Information Centre, University of Reading.

Tizard, B. and Hughes, M. (1984) *Young Children Learning: Talking and thinking at home and at school*, Fontana.

Dear

I hope you are well. I am writing to let you know that I am in Greendale Hospital. Last week, I didn't look where I was going properly, and I bumped my head on a big tree. The doctors and nurses have put a bandage on me and they say I will be better soon, but I have to stay in hospital for one more week.

When you go to nursery/school tomorrow, do you think you could write me a letter with all your news, or make me a get well card? That would be lovely!

Love from,

Postman Pat.

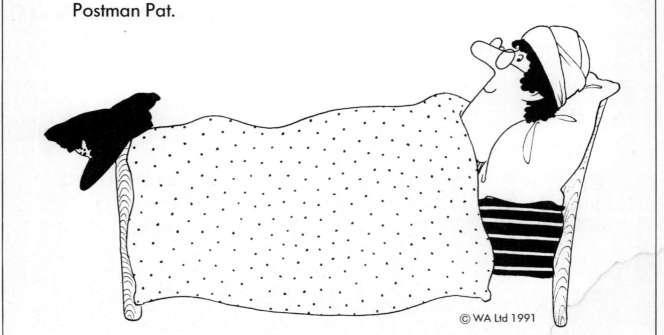

© WA Ltd 1991

What's on?, see page 38

We've got one of those!, see page 43

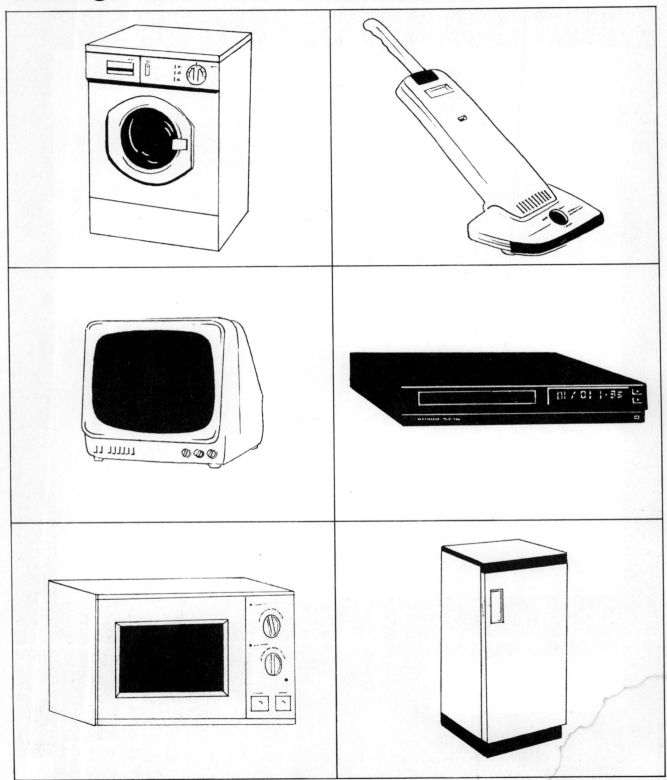

Enjoys a favourite story repeated

Looks at books with friends

Looks at books alone

Knows where front of book starts

Aware that print is read

Enjoys listening to story at school

Turns over pages one at a time

Enjoys story at home

Can retell part of story using pictures

Finger goes left to right over print (not matching)

Good memory for story

Can retell whole story using pictures

Uses 'book' language when retells story

Can recognise letters from own name in print

READING

Name .... D.O.B ....

(Devised by Caroline Matusiak, 'Shared Records', *Child Education*, November 1988.)

Favourite five, see page 82

If I were going to the moon, these are my favourite five books that I would take with me.

Concepts about print: test, see page 84

Concepts about print score sheet

Name:_____ Age: _____ Date: _____

Recorder:_____ Date of birth:_____ Test score: ____ /24

Page	Score	Item	Comment
Cover		1. Front of book	
		2. Print contains message	
		3. Where to start	
		4. Which way to go	
		5. Return sweep to left	
		6. Word by word matching	
		7. First and last concept	
		8. Bottom of picture	
		9. Begin at the new top left-hand corner of the text, or turn book around	
		10. Line order altered	
		11. Left page before right	
		12. One change in word order	
		13. One change in letter order	
		14. One change in letter order	
		15. Meaning of question mark	
		16. Meaning of full stop	
		17. Meaning of comma	
		18. Meaning of quotation marks	
		19. Locate lower case letters when shown upper case (T t B b)	
		20. Reversible words was, no	
		21. One letter: two letters	
		22. One word: two words	
		23. First and last letter of word	
		24. Capital letter	

(From *The Early Detection of Reading Difficulties* by Marie Clay, Heinemann Educational, 1989.)

This page may be photocopied for use in the classroom and should not be declared in any return in respect of any photocopying licence.

Running records, see page 85

Summary of running record

Name: _____ Date: _____ Date of birth: _____ Age: _____
Recorder: _____

SUMMARY OF RUNNING ERRORS

	Text titles	Total words / error	Error rate	Accuracy	Self-correction rate
1. Easy	_____	_____	1:_____	_____%	1:_____
2. Instructional	_____	_____	1:_____	_____%	1:_____
3. Hard	_____	_____	1:_____	_____%	1:_____

Directional movement _____

ANALYSIS OF ERRORS Cues used and cues neglected

Easy _____
Instructional _____
_____
Hard _____
_____

Cross checking on cues

Page		E	SC	Cues used (M, S or V) E SC

Key: E = Error; SC = Self-correction; M = Meaning; S = Structure; V = Visual.

(From *The Early Detection of Reading Difficulties* by Marie Clay, Heinemann Educational 1981.)

Miscue made simple, see page 86

Name _____ Age _____

Title and page(s) of book _____ Class _____

_____ Year _____

Date _____

Substitutions

	Word printed	Word read	Similarity			
			Sound	Look	Part of speech	Meaning
1						
2						
3						
4						
5						
6						
7						
8						
9						
10						
11						
12						

Tally of refusals	

Negative miscue rate = $\dfrac{\text{Meaning errors + refusals}}{\text{Total number of words read}} \times 100 = \qquad \times 100$

$= \qquad \%$

Level = Independent/instructional/frustration
        (1%)   (5%)   (10%)

Notes on miscue analysis

(From *Assessing Reading Strategies at Key Stage 1* by Cliff Moon, Reading and Language Centre, University of Reading, 1991.)